Liturgy and the New Evangelization

Liturgy and the New Evangelization

Practicing the Art of Self-Giving Love

Timothy P. O'Malley

LITURGICAL PRESS

Collegeville, Minnesota

www.litpress.org

1   2   3   4   5   6   7   8   9

Library of Congress Cataloging-in-Publication Data

O'Malley, Timothy P.
    Liturgy and the new evangelization : practicing the art of self-giving love / Timothy P. O'Malley.
      pages cm
    Includes bibliographical references.
    ISBN 978-0-8146-3764-7 — ISBN 978-0-8146-3789-0 (ebook)
      1. Evangelicalism—Catholic Church.   2. Catholic Church—Liturgy.
    3. Liturgical adaptation—Catholic Church.   I. Title.

BX1397.O43   2014
264'.02—dc23   2013037432

In gratitude to my wife,
Kara,
who has taught me to live the nuptial liturgy
each day of our married life.

Contents

Introduction

The gift of "real" love is something that each human being desires. We first know this love while gazing into the eyes of our parents. We seek authentic friendships, ones in which a communion of souls takes place. We desire romantic love, to encounter another human being whose beauty and goodness is transformative of our identity. We are made to love, to give ourselves away as a response to the gift we have already received.

Whatever the new evangelization is, it is incomprehensible outside the domain of love. Not simply the love of one human being for another, though such love is indeed *very* good. Rather, the church's mission of the new evangelization is coming to perceive anew the logic of self-giving love revealed in Jesus Christ; a revelation of divine love that expands our imaginations regarding the possibility of what human love could become when knit into the triune God's own life.[1] A love made manifest in the life of the church, in those disciples filled with joy who have become members of the Body of Christ: "As the Father has loved me, so I have loved you; abide in my love. If you keep my commandments, you will abide in my love, just as I have kept my Father's commandments and abide in his love. I have said these things to you so that my joy may be in you, and that your joy may be complete" (John 15:9-11).[2] The new evangelization, for this reason, is nothing less than a recommitment to God's own pedagogy of love as mediated through the church's ministries of proclamation, prayer, and mission.

Because the new evangelization is fundamentally a renewal of the church's eyes of love, it must be liturgical. Of course, this claim can easily be misunderstood. The liturgical context of the new evangelization is not simply an affirmation of the centrality of liturgy in the church's life. Instead, what I mean to propose is that the practices of the church's liturgical rites function in such a way that they are to inform every aspect of the church's mission of the new evangelization. For in liturgical rites, we do not only consider the love of God as a theoretical possibility but we *participate* in such

1

love through visible signs and words. Our desires and hopes, our sorrows and tears, are taken up into God's own life and made into a spiritual offering. In such moments, we allow God's own gift of love to be written upon the contours of our bodies, now given over to the world as a sacramental offering: "present your bodies as a living sacrifice, holy and acceptable to God, which is your spiritual worship. Do not be conformed to this world, but be transformed by the renewal of your minds, so that you may discern what is the will of God—what is good and acceptable and perfect" (Rom 12:1-2). As long as the purpose of the new evangelization is humanity's partaking in the self-giving love of God, then liturgical prayer is integral to this "new evangelization."

This book ultimately has three purposes relative to articulating the liturgical task of the new evangelization. First, it seeks to develop a liturgical and thus theological argument about the nature of the new evangelization. The new evangelization is not simply about the adoption of novel pastoral programs, the cultivation of small-group faith sharing, the strengthening of Catholic identity in schools and parishes, the use of social media in spreading the Gospel, or a renewed confidence in performing public professions of faith. These are instruments that are part of a larger narrative, one that has yet to be fully articulated. As the *Lineamenta* for the Synod on the New Evangelization states:

> Presently, in reviewing the dynamics of the "new evangelization," the expression can now be applied to the Church's renewed efforts to meet the challenges which today's society and cultures, in view of the significant changes taking place, are posing to the Christian faith, its proclamation and its witness. In facing these challenges, the Church does not give up or retreat into herself; instead, she undertakes a project to revitalize herself. She makes the Person of Jesus Christ and a personal encounter with him central to her thinking, knowing that he will give his Spirit and provide the force to announce and proclaim the Gospel in new ways which can speak to today's cultures.[3]

The new evangelization becomes in this case a transformation of all culture, of all human existence, spurred on by an encounter with Christ himself. Indeed, in every generation, the church must perform a "new evangelization," seeking to incarnate the Christian faith anew, to recommence the divine-human exchange that has defined Christian history. And in this way, the grammar of liturgical prayer can help the church better understand how to carry out the new evangelization as a form of self-giving love.

The second purpose of this book relates to the renewal of both liturgical practice and formation. In the postconciliar years, a kind of positivism has developed relative to the formative nature of liturgical prayer. Simply, we have assumed that the performance of rites and subsequent reflection upon liturgical practice will lead to certain intellectual and spiritual dispositions. The one who participates in the liturgy will have a solid grasp of the salvific narrative manifested in the Bible, of the spiritual practice of psalmody, of a robust theology of baptism, etc. Often, as liturgists, we have allowed ourselves to shape specific decisions regarding liturgical practice in order to communicate an idea, a principle, which we view as essential to the Christian life. Against such a claim, I hope to demonstrate that the "formative" potential of liturgical prayer in the modern context remains a rather elusive reality.

For example, few ritual activities within Catholicism are more exemplary of this complicated process of liturgical formation than the rite of infant baptism. This rite performs certain theological and cultural claims of Catholicism regarding this sacrament.[4] The preferred place and time of baptism is within the Easter Vigil or Sunday eucharistic liturgy so as to bring out the paschal quality of the sacrament.[5] The theological imagery surrounding infant baptism within the rite is becoming a child of God, being enlightened, as well as washing away the effects of original sin. The responsibility for the developing faith of the infant is placed in the hands of the parents and godparents, and the gathered assembly.[6] Yet, as any pastoral minister is aware, the cultural meaning "communicated" through the rite of baptism is not necessarily the same act of meaning created by its participants. The presider of the sacrament may choose one series of prayers within the rite over another, emphasizing a baptismal theology that resonates with his preferred interpretation of the sacrament. The couple baptizing their child may miss this subtle theological move by the priest or deacon, instead conceiving of baptism as a formal acknowledgement of new life, a rite of passage performed by the church but ultimately about family and tradition. One pair of grandparents may express gratitude that their grandchild has been rescued from the flames of hell, while the other may see some sadness upon this occasion, since their once-Jewish daughter has promised to raise her child within the church. The assembly will have a similar range of meanings, from a sense of paschal joy at seeing new members entering into the Body of Christ, to boredom and annoyance that yet another interruption to Mass has occurred. If the ministers within the church desire a fruitful reception of the sacrament on the part of the infant, one that involves both an understanding of the official theology of the rite by the parents and godparents, as well as a way of life that has become baptismal within the family and the assembly, the ministers will need to be cognizant of the official theology of the rite; the presumed dispositions necessary for fruitful reception and participation within the sacrament by the various parties; and, the already acquired dispositions that act as lens through which the official meaning of the sacramental rite must pass.

Thus, if one is to perform a liturgical education that is evangelical, transformative of history, culture, and each individual life, then the church must dedicate itself to discerning anew that *savoir faire* necessary for teaching Christians the art of liturgical prayer in our own age. Catholicism's new evangelization is an opportune time to examine practices of formation in light of present cultural realities (some of which are opposed to the pedagogy of divine love performed in the church's liturgical rites). Liturgical formation in the new evangelization will include much more than reflection upon one's own experience of a specific rite. Instead, such liturgical formation will enable one to engage in liturgical activity; to participate in liturgical prayer in such a way that one's very attitude toward human life itself is transformed.

Lastly, this book attends to the wisdom implicit in the liturgical practice of the church. That is, while liturgical prayer may not *immediately* instill certain intellectual and spiritual dispositions, such prayer does seek to *gradually* form us in a liturgical approach to human life: to work and marriage, to art and beauty, to education and leisure, to politics and justice. As Jean Corbon notes in his classic text, *The Wellspring of Worship*:

> If the liturgy is the mystery of the river of life that streams from the Father and the Lamb and if it reaches us and draws us when we celebrate it, then it does so in order that it may water our entire life and render it fruitful. The eternal liturgy in which the economy of salvation reaches completion "is accomplished" by us in our sacramental celebrations in order that it may in turn be accomplished in us, in the least fibers of our being and of our human community.[7]

When we begin to understand how liturgical practice transfigures our imaginations, our desires, everything that it means to be human, then we will begin to see the concrete ways that the wisdom of liturgical prayer may overflow into our own existence here and now. How participation in the liturgical rites of the church gradually inspires the Christian toward a mysticism of the ordinary, to an offering of the return gift of our very lives as an act of love.

This book will consist of five chapters. First, I will unfold a liturgical theology of evangelization in chapter 1. This liturgical theology begins with an analysis of "evangelization" as it is treated in three key documents: Paul VI's *Evangelium Nuntiandi*, John Paul II's *Catechesi Tradendae*, and lastly the *General Directory for Catechesis*. Having set up a working definition of evangelization, the substance of chapter 1 is a re-reading of *Sacrosanctum Concilium* in light of the theme of liturgical evangelization. Liturgical prayer is evangelical insofar as it enables one to participate in God's self-giving love, capacitating each Christian to offer him or herself for the transfiguration of history, culture, and each human relationship through the paschal mystery. In the second chapter, I turn toward an analysis of those cultural obstacles in the United States that necessitate a new evangelization relative to liturgical prayer. In the United States, the primary context of our prayer is a form of secularization, aptly called "Moralistic Therapeutic Deism" by the sociologist Christian Smith. Such an approach to religious understanding is particularly problematic when considering what it means to participate fully, consciously, and actively in the liturgical prayer of the church. Moralistic Therapeutic Deism effects this participation in three major ways in the United States, including a thinning of the Christian's imagination, a decreased desire toward a deeper understanding of the rites, and an exclusive focus upon individual flourishing. If the liturgical prayer of the church is to become a site of this new evangelization, then these issues must be addressed strategically in the church's pastoral approach to liturgical formation.

In the final three chapters, I outline strategic areas relative to performing the church's mission of the new evangelization relative to liturgical prayer. The first area includes a commitment to fostering the imagination of the Christian through a deeper attention to the proclamation of the narrative of salvation, the promotion of the liturgical homily. The second area is dedicated to renewing within the Catholic imagination an integral link between liturgical prayer and vocation. And the third considers "rites of return," focusing less on those who are returning to the church and more upon what is waiting for them in the church's liturgical life.

This essay in liturgical evangelization will not address every facet of how liturgical prayer is integral to the new evangelization. But the hope is that the reader might encounter in this text a renewal of one's own imagination regarding the formative and thus transformative potential of liturgical prayer in the life of the church. For such prayer is not intended as either an aesthetic exercise in presenting the mystery of God through signs, nor an effective pedagogical tool for promoting one form of ideology above another. Rather, liturgical prayer seeks to elevate our humanity into the very life of God, teaching us over the course of our lifetimes what it means to practice the art of self-giving love. Such a formation is not intended for the renewal of the church's prayer alone but as a gift to the whole cosmos; as a way of incarnating within both our individual and communal history the radically disruptive fact that God is love.

In an introduction to a book on the new evangelization, it also seems prudent to include some biographical note regarding my own formation. I am a Roman Catholic theologian, whose first encounter with both the intellectual and spiritual life of the church occurred in the context of the postconciliar liturgical rites to which I am deeply committed today. Growing up in the Diocese of Knoxville, in which Catholics are definitively a minority, the Catholic liturgical imagination stood out against the backdrop of other Christian traditions. Traveling with fellow youth to monasteries (as we did every summer), encountering the Office of the church at a young age, I came to see how every aspect of our humanity is offered up in liturgical prayer. I owe the monks of St. Bernard's Abbey in Cullman, Alabama a note of thanks for this insight.

At the University of Notre Dame, where I did my undergraduate and master's work, I learned to study the liturgy as a source of theological and spiritual insight. I learned from John Cavadini, David Fagerberg, Maxwell Johnson, and Nathan Mitchell the importance of the liturgical-sacramental life to the theological enterprise. My own doctoral work at Boston College, focusing on liturgical-sacramental theology, spirituality, and preaching, renewed my imagination regarding how to write and teach persuasively and truthfully about liturgical prayer. Here, my gratitude extends to the thoughtful guidance of Khaled Anatolios, John Baldovin, S.J., Thomas Groome, Paul Kolbet, Bruce Morrill, S.J., and Jane Regan. While at Boston College, located in a city that has grown tired of the mystery of Catholicism, which suffers from the wounds of an institution that committed so many sins against its members, I began to recognize the need for a new evangelization: an evangelization that seeks to recapture the imagination and the desires of the faithful regarding what takes place in the liturgical rites of the church.

I then returned to the University of Notre Dame, taking up directorship of the Notre Dame Center for Liturgy. Here, in teaching undergraduates, I came to recognize their own incapacity (at least for some of them) to see liturgical prayer as anything more than a public celebration of what a certain community thinks about the world. Equally so, they expressed to me suspicions regarding Catholicism, doubts about the validity of doctrine, tradition, and prescribed prayer forms. In some ways, this work was written with these students in mind; it is an attempt to offer a persuasive, and I hope true, vision of liturgical prayer that is not a subjugation of our humanity to rules and regulations. Liturgical prayer is instead the opportunity to lift up the deepest desires of our hearts to the Father through the Son in the unity of the Holy Spirit.

I cannot help but conclude with a note of gratitude to two dear friends. Leonard DeLorenzo, a co-worker at the Institute for Church Life, gave me my first opportunity to articulate a rather sophisticated, and perhaps too heady, version of a sacramental theology of gift to high school students in the Notre Dame Vision program—one of the many vocation initiatives inaugurated through the generosity of the Lilly Endowment. He also encouraged me to teach a course for Notre Dame undergraduates who serve as mentors-in-faith in this program, allowing me to further articulate a comprehensive vision of what constitutes the liturgical life of self-gift. I owe the substance of this work, its structure, and the pattern of speech, to what I have learned through Lenny's graciousness toward my work, not to mention countless conversations about the eucharistic shape of Christian vocation. Lastly, I would like to thank Kara, my beloved wife. A youth minister, a director of Christian formation, and now a stay-at-home catechist, Kara has formed me (the academic) to think about the pastoral life of the church. Further, during our years of marriage, of struggling to have a child, and then finally adopting in 2012, I have learned more from Kara about what constitutes the eucharistic vocation of marriage than from any text I have read or written. This work, despite its foibles and follies, is dedicated to her.

A Liturgical Theology of Evangelization

Speaking about "evangelization" in Catholic circles often requires a bit of care on the part of the educator. The cultural imagination perceives evangelization as a synonym for proselytizing: convincing co-workers, friends, and neighbors through guilt and subtle coercion to join one's parish or congregation. A Catholic community in Massachusetts that carried out an assessment of strengths and weaknesses in its common life reacted with relief when informed that its major weakness was a failure to evangelize. In graduate seminars in catechetics, the topic of evangelization often requires numerous class sessions devoted to defending the use of the term. In the media, the term "evangelical" refers less to the proclamation of the Gospel, the transformation of all facets of human culture in light of Christ, and more to defined political commitments.

The reticence toward using the term "evangelization" is at least partially influenced by Christians whose belief systems have been formed by the American privatization of religion that treats benign tolerance as a necessary public virtue (see chapter 2). Even more so, the discomfort with using evangelization to describe the mission of the church reveals forgetfulness of the church's very identity: the self-giving love of Jesus Christ (which is the very life of the triune God), now suffusing the church. Only when the sacramental nature of evangelization is remembered will the term become palatable, even persuasive to Catholics. And this deeper, theological nature of evangelization is best discovered through the liturgical life of the church.

This initial chapter seeks to restore a "Catholic" understanding of evangelization, one that is intrinsic to the liturgical renewal called for by the Second Vatican Council. Evangelization is not a political ideology smuggled in using theological language. It is the church's mission to give of itself out of the depths of love for the renewal of the world.

Thus, this chapter will consist of two parts. First, I define evangelization with particular attention to postconciliar documents on evangelization. Second, I discern how a robust definition of evangelization is not simply implicit but intrinsic to the liturgical renewal enacted at the Second Vatican Council.

What Is Evangelization?

Falling in love is often a surprise, a moment in our lives in which our history is rewritten by the good news that we are indeed loved. The revelation of love reconfigures what we once thought were our priorities in life. The stories that we tell change as our individual journey is now knit into another's. I remember that when I first fell in love with my wife, I could not help but mention her name with near comic regularity in each conversation I had with friends and family alike. As we grow into this love in the context of marriage, the name of our husband or wife takes on the contours of our common narrative, of the maturing love that we have embodied in specific times and places. For me, to say the name "Kara" is not simply to utter four letters, consisting of two syllables, a word whose root is the Latin *caritas*; instead, this name recalls the person of my wife, the sorrows and joys that we shared as our mutual love has slowly formed us over the last decade.

This transformation of our identity through falling in love is perhaps even better represented in having a child. The joys of sleeping until one wakes up naturally, of leisurely weekend brunches, and of maximizing efficiency in work and home life is traded for restless nights, speedy meals while a son or daughter is sleeping, and an ever-changing routine dependent upon a newborn's needs. The surprise, of course, is not that having a child changes one's life, reconfiguring once sacrosanct schedules and rituals. Instead, it is that even the least palatable tasks become a kind of delight, an offering of love from parent to child. Becoming a parent is encountering the gift of love itself, a love so remarkable that our response is nothing less than total self-gift.

In order to understand what the church means by evangelization, it is essential that one grasp such moments of self-gift, of authentic encounter with the beloved. Evangelization is the grammar of the church's love, the nuptial speech of those who have encountered the love of God in Jesus Christ, a love sacramentally manifested in the church. Such love, the Christian dares to hope, not only transfigures our individual life but every aspect of history and society. The nature of evangelization as love may be found, at least implicitly, in those ecclesial documents that treat the term. It is to an exegesis of such documents that we now turn.

Reading Ecclesial Documents: A Method

Quoting ecclesial documents easily can become a tiresome affair—a gathering of authoritative proof texts to back up one's particular claims. Such an approach to reading church documents inundates the reader with quotes, failing to make a particular argument regarding what the text means. Thus, if I am to define how evangelization is fundamentally a matter of self-giving love learned in the school of the Christ, most perfectly embodied in the liturgical-sacramental life of the church, it will require a *theological* approach to reading such documents. Church documents use shorthand, key phrases from previous theological inquiry to communicate a vision to the universal church. An astute reading of these documents often requires deeper attention to the theological wellspring, the very sources of thought that are implicit in the text. Through this theological approach, one comes to see that the term evangelization is nothing less than shorthand for how the church is to relate to the world, an expression of an ecclesiology that seeks the redemption of all humanity through the agapic pedagogy of the church.

Evangelium Nuntiandi

In 1974, the Synod of Bishops considered the theme of evangelization in the modern context, a concern arising from the Second Vatican Council's concern "to make the Church of the twentieth century ever better fitted for proclaiming the Gospel to the people of the twentieth century."[1] The synod acknowledged three guiding concerns: the failure of the Gospel to have a powerful effect on the human conscience in the modern world; the Gospel's relative impoverishment in transforming human society in modernity; and a discernment of those methods most apt for performing evangelization in the twentieth century (EN 4). The document is clear that a renewal of the church's ministry of proclamation is not a luxury but a "duty incumbent on her by the command of the Lord Jesus, so that people can believe and be saved" (EN 5).

As such, evangelization must begin from its christological center, from Christ who is the preeminent evangelist. Jesus Christ proclaims the Kingdom of God as an interruption of our limited notions of power and prestige (EN 8), the announcement of a liberating salvation that re-orients life toward the Father (EN 9), the radical interior conversion made possible through the self-giving love of Christ on the cross (EN 10), and the suasive and re-velatory preaching and deeds of the Word made flesh (EN 11). The church receives her mission of evangelization through her union with Christ; that is, the community of the evangelized (those who have given themselves over to the prodigal logic of the kingdom of God) becomes evangelizers. Evangelization is not simply peripheral to the church's identity, an option for the committed. Instead, as Paul VI notes:

> Evangelizing is in fact the grace and vocation proper to the Church, her deepest identity. She exists in order to evangelize, that is to say in order to preach and teach, to be the channel of the gift of grace, to reconcile sinners with God, and to perpetuate Christ's sacrifice in the Mass, which is the memorial of his death and glorious Resurrection. (EN 14)

The entire mission of the church, its lived ecclesiology, is that of evangelization. The church gives itself over to its deepest identity as the beloved of Christ, letting its message infuse every part of the church's ministry.

Thus, evangelization is nothing less than shorthand for the church's mission of preaching, of catechesis, of sacramental ministry, and the deeds of love its members perform for the transfiguration of the world (EN 17). Such a process of evangelization is both transformative of the individual and society as a whole. Paul VI writes:

> For the church, evangelizing means bringing the Good News into all the strata of humanity, and through its influence transforming humanity from within and making it new: "Now I am making the whole of creation new." But there is no new humanity if there are not first of all new persons renewed by Baptism and by lives lived according to the Gospel. The purpose of evangelization is therefore precisely this interior change, and if it had to be expressed in one sentence the best way of stating it would be to say that the Church evangelizes when she seeks to convert, solely through the divine power of the Message she proclaims, both the personal and collective consciences of people, the activities in which they engage, and the lives and concrete milieus which are theirs. (EN 18)

One can see that evangelization is no minor task. It is not reducible to pastoral programs, inviting Catholics to return to the church; to door-to-door preaching, proliferating Catholic thought through blogs, or inviting a co-worker to come to Mass (although, it may in fact involve such pastoral care and practice). Instead, evangelization is the transformation of all humanity, of all culture, of all society through an encounter with Christ: "of affecting and as it were upsetting, through the power of the Gospel, mankind's criteria of judgment, determining values, points of interest, lines of thought, sources of inspiration and models of life, which are in contrast with the Word of God and the plan of salvation" (EN 19). When the church is truly evangelical, it seeks to invite all of humanity to consider the Good News that salvation in Christ elevates what it means to be human—both individually and socially. Catholicism is an intrinsically evangelical faith insofar as it seeks not to promote its own bureaucratic structures but the union of all humanity in Christ. As Henri de Lubac writes, "Humanity is one, organically one by its divine structure; it the Church's mission to reveal to men that pristine unity that they have lost, to restore and complete it." [2] Evangelization requires a contemplation of the church's narrative of salvation by believers, a self-examination of the interior life of those of us who are disciples of Christ, and an invitation offered to others to participate in that peaceful union of humanity and God enacted in the church's life.

Therefore, the mere memorization or knowledge of the church's doctrine, her creedal statements, her liturgical regulations and moral wisdom is not adequate for evangelization. The knowledge of such doctrine, of the liturgical life of the church, or the moral teaching that elevates human action toward the divine life, should become incarnate in family life, in human work, in politics and society, in art and leisure (EN 28–29). The doctrine of the incarnation becomes evangelical when it moves from expressing a historical idea from a distant past, to a manifestation of the enfleshment of the divine Word in the human condition, a realization that inevitably leads one to ponder what it means to be human. The liturgical life of the church becomes evangelical when the liturgical and sacramental rites of the church cease being performed in a perfunctory manner, but re-inscribe human life as a divine offering of love to the Father through the Son in the unity of the Spirit. The moral life, commitment to justice and charity at both the local and global level, moves from being a humanistic concern to an evangelical commitment when the individual sees his or her deeds of love as witnessing to the God who first loved us.

While the document treats other aspects of evangelization more extensively, the animating vision of the text is the transformation of human society, of life, of culture itself through the mediation of those Christians who have fallen so deeply in love with Jesus in the school of the church that their existence becomes part of the renewal of the world. Not because Christians hate the world, seeking to promote a sectarian mindset. Rather, the church can contemplate humanity, with all of its light and darkness, all of its sin and hope, through the icon of Christ. Jesus Christ embodies what we may become if we give ourselves over to the Word made flesh:

> may the world of our time, which is searching, sometimes with anguish,
> sometimes with hope, be enabled to receive the Good News not from

evangelizers who are dejected, discouraged, impatient or anxious, but from ministers of the Gospel whose lives glow with fervor, who have first received the joy of Christ, and who are willing to risk their lives so that the Kingdom may be proclaimed and the Church established in the midst of the world. (EN 80)

The vision of evangelization, set out by Paul VI, is the process of divinization whereby our humanity, our society, every facet of human culture is gradually knit into the peace of the reign of God. The evangelizer, the one who seeks to serve as a medium of this transformation, operates out of the depths of Christian love, "the love of a father; and again, it is the love of mother. It is this love that the Lord expects from every preacher of the Gospel, from every builder of the Church . . . the concern to give the truth and to bring people into unity" (EN 79). Commitment to the mission of evangelization is a return-gift to the God who first loved us.

In conclusion, the church's commitment to evangelization is not a sectarian strategy by those seeking to coerce the culture to believe in the Gospel at all costs. Rather, the turn to evangelization in the postconciliar years is an authentic, ecclesiological consequence of the understanding of the church articulated by the documents of the Second Vatican Council. As *Lumen Gentium* (LG) notes, "All are called to this catholic unity of the people of God which prefigures and promotes universal peace. And to it belong, or are related in different ways: the catholic faithful, ones who believe in Christ, and finally all of humankind, called by God's grace to salvation." [3] The church evangelizes not out of a sense of hubris but in light of her deepest identity as "a sacrament—a sign and instrument, that is, of communion with God and of the unity of the entire human race" (LG 1). At the origin of evangelization is the eucharistic nature of the church, seeking to draw all of humanity into one body, precisely that all of humanity may commune with the living God in peace. As Joseph Ratzinger writes:

> The content of the Eucharist, what happens in it, is the uniting of Christians, bringing them from their state of separation into the unity of the one Bread and the one Body. The Eucharist is thus understood entirely in a dynamic ecclesiological perspective. It is the living process through which, time and again, the Church's activity of becoming Church takes place. [4]

The eucharistic nature of evangelization means that the process of evangelization, of inviting all of humanity into a relationship with Christ, must be carried out as a sacramental action of gratitude, a return-gift to the living God for the love that we have first received.

Catechesi Tradendae

Integrally linked to the church's mission of evangelization is catechesis. I have often heard fellow theologians refer derisively to "mere catechesis" in contradistinction to forms of theological inquiry expected at the university level. Such disdain for catechesis among theological thinkers makes sense if catechesis is understood as nothing more than a form of elementary indoctrination into Catholic faith. Yet John Paul II's *Catechesi Tradendae* (CT), emerging out of the Synod of Bishops held in October 1977, offers a robust understanding of catechesis, one related to the eucharistic approach to evangelization described above. Though there is some overlap between *Evangelium Nuntiandi* and *Catechesi Tradendae*, it is profitable for defining a liturgical theology for the new evangelization to treat one particular facet of this document related to evangelization: the christocentric nature of catechesis as foundational to the transformation of human experience, a pedagogical claim embodied most perfectly in the liturgical life of the church.

Before treating this theme, I should first note how this document approaches the relationship between catechesis and evangelization. Defining catechesis, John Paul II writes, "catechesis is an education of children, young people and adults in the faith, which includes especially the teaching of Christian doctrine imparted, generally speaking, in an organic and systematic way, with a view to initiating the hearers into the fullness of Christian life." [5] Importantly, the ministry of catechesis is systematic in scope, yet necessarily emerging from a deeper encounter with Christian faith through the initial proclamation of the kerygma, through preaching, through Christian life, the sacraments, and witness. For this reason, catechesis is perceived as one moment in the larger ecology of the church's mission of evangelization; it is a moment of maturation, following initial proclamation.

Of course, the document recognizes that the pastoral reality of the day means that catechesis often ends up fulfilling a variety of moments in the church's ministry of evangelization. Those who are to receive catechesis are many times marginally connected to the church, baptized but never catechized, or catechized so poorly that they are not yet capable of entering more deeply into the mystery of Christ (CT 19). In such instances, catechesis must necessarily involve itself "not only with nourishing and teaching the

faith but also with rousing it unceasingly with the help of grace, with opening the heart, with converting, and with preparing total adherence to Jesus
Christ on the part of those who are still on the threshold of faith" (CT 19).

As a privileged moment of evangelization, catechesis may stand as a
part for the whole, providing a more systematic understanding of the task
of evangelization. At the very heart of catechesis, according to the document, is Jesus Christ:

> The primary and essential object of catechesis is, to use an expression
> dear to Saint Paul and also to contemporary theology, "the mystery of
> Christ." Catechizing is a way to lead a person to study this Mystery in
> all its dimensions. . . . It is therefore to reveal in the Person of Christ
> the whole of God's eternal design reaching fulfillment in that Person.
> It is to seek to understand the meaning of Christ's actions and words
> and of the signs worked by him, for they simultaneously hide and
> reveal his mystery. Accordingly, the definitive aim of catechesis is to
> put people not only in touch but in communion, in intimacy, with Jesus
> Christ: only he can lead us to the love of the Father in the Spirit and
> make us share in the life of the Holy Trinity. (CT 5)

When the document affirms that Christ is the center of catechesis, it means
something more nuanced than the person and works of Jesus are central
to a catechetical curriculum. Catechesis is a sacramental activity, one in
which the catechist uses words and signs, including his or her own person,
to point toward the reality of God. Catechists are to offer their words, their
teaching, their very selves, allowing them to become not simply personal
expressions of doctrine or the Scriptures, but an iconic glimpse into the
self-giving love of the Father and the Son; an act of teaching in which the
Holy Spirit comes to dwell among us. For this reason, the christocentricity
of catechesis already points toward a liturgical or doxological encounter
with Christ: "This teaching is not a body of abstract truths. It is the communication of the living mystery of God" (CT 7).

To a certain extent, the claim that catechesis involves an encounter with
Christ may sound rather unsurprising to the contemporary reader. Yet, what
is meant by John Paul II when he states that the final end of catechesis is
communion with Christ? Turning to *Redemptoris Hominis*, written shortly
before *Catechesi Tradendae*, one discovers why John Paul II places so much
emphasis on catechesis as a transforming encounter with the mystery of
God in Christ Jesus. He writes:

> The Church's fundamental function in every age and particularly in ours is to direct [our] gaze, to point the awareness and experience of the whole of humanity towards the mystery of God, to help all . . . to be familiar with the profundity of the Redemption taking place in Christ Jesus. At the same time [our] deepest sphere is involved—we mean the sphere of human hearts, consciences and events.[6]

Jesus Christ is not simply an exemplary model of human conduct; rather, in Christ Jesus, humanity comes face-to-face with the love of God poured out for the salvation of the world. Catechesis is the art of systematic amazement, one in which humanity ponders the depths of divine love through concentrated attention to Christ's life manifested in the church's ministries of proclamation, of liturgy, of service, and prayer. This divine revelation does not deny our humanity, forcing us beyond time and history. The church's catechesis is necessarily humanistic, committed to a sober imagining of the possibilities of what our common humanity might become in Christ. In fact, the church is the very humanity of Christ working in the present day. Jean Mouroux, commenting on this aspect of the church, states:

> Just as Christ's humanity was once visible as the efficacious sign of the mystery of salvation, so the Church has its own humanity as the efficacious sign of the same saving mystery. Christian existence is essentially spiritual, being based on an *esse spirituale*, grace; but, as communicated to human beings by the God-Man, it comes to us by way of the body, and is made effective in us by means of signs. The divine agape was first communicated through Christ's Humanity; it is now communicated through the Humanity of the Church.[7]

The christocentric nature of catechesis is not simply a declaration that, indeed, Jesus Christ is the central figure of Christianity. Christocentricity is a robust affirmation that catechesis is an unfolding of the divine mystery of redemption, one that takes place in *this day*. The process of redemption includes all that it means to be human, precisely because the central concern of catechesis is to enter into communion with the Word made flesh. Catechesis is evangelical insofar as it "aims therefore at developing understanding of the mystery of Christ in the light of God's word, so that the whole of a person's humanity is impregnated by that word" (CT 20). The imagination, the intellect, the deepest desires of the human heart come to be understood in light of the divine love revealed in Christ.

Implicit to this understanding of catechesis as a moment of evangelization is an approach to liturgical prayer as an evangelical ministry of the church. As the document states, "catechesis is intrinsically linked with the whole of liturgical and sacramental activity, for it is in the sacraments, especially in the Eucharist, that Christ Jesus works in fullness for the transformation of human beings" (CT 23). Liturgical prayer contributes to the catechetical, and thus evangelical, mission of the church not because it is offers a pedagogically effective way of teaching complex doctrines or acquainting Catholics with the basic narrative of the Scriptures. Liturgical prayer is the very divine-human exchange, which the catechetical ministry of the church hopes to deepen through systematic instruction. As *Sacrosanctum Concilium* (SC) makes clear, the liturgy of the church (especially the Eucharist) "is supremely effective in enabling the faithful to express in their lives and portray to others the mystery of Christ and the real nature of the true church" (SC 2). Liturgical prayer is an encounter with the very reality of Christ, the God-Man who elevates our human nature to divine life.

Thus, *Catechesi Tradendae* prescribes a doxological form of catechesis, whereby the Christian slowly assimilates the mystery of Christ into a way of life through a systematic instruction that is transformative of human experience. This assimilation into the christological mystery is essential to the evangelical nature of catechesis, whereby each particular human being, and thus slowly each culture is impregnated by the Word. In John Paul II's description of catechesis as christocentric, we have already begun to contemplate the liturgical task of evangelization. Liturgical prayer is the living of Christ's own life, the mystery of divine self-gift taking place through the offering of orations to the Father, through the marking of time in the liturgical year, through stained glass windows, and incense rising above altars. The very mystery of Christ wonderfully contemplated in catechesis, is even more remarkably written upon the human body through liturgical prayer.[8]

General Directory for Catechesis

The *General Directory for Catechesis* (GDC) is a mature summation of the church's thinking about evangelization, specifically related to catechesis. Nonetheless, as will become obvious, the document provides further evidence (albeit underdeveloped) that the liturgical life of the church is integral to the work of evangelization. Because of the document's consideration of liturgical education within the sphere of evangelization, I will devote some attention to it before treating more fully a liturgical theology of evangelization drawn from *Sacrosanctum Concilium*.

The *General Directory for Catechesis*, published in 1997, is an updating of an earlier document (*General Catechetical Directory* [1971]). In this earlier directory, the topic of evangelization receives scant attention. Where the document mentions evangelization, it presents it solely as a preliminary task to catechesis.[9] By the time of the *General Directory for Catechesis*, evangelization was no longer relegated to a preparatory phase for systematic catechesis. Instead, the ministry of catechesis is located squarely within the domain of evangelization. Drawing from the Constitution on Divine Revelation (*Dei Verbum*), the Directory notes:

> God, in his greatness, uses a pedagogy to reveal himself to the human person: he uses human events and words to communicate his plan; he does so progressively and in stages, so as to draw ever closer to man. God, in fact, operates in such a manner that man comes to knowledge of his salvific plan by means of the events of salvation history and the inspired words which accompany and explain them.[10]

Divine revelation is structured pedagogically. God, like a master pedagogue, uses signs and deeds to reveal to humanity the divine plan for all of existence. Evangelization, employing this very same divine pedagogy, "transmits Revelation to the world . . . brought about in words and deeds. It is at once testimony and proclamation, word and sacrament, teaching and task" (GDC 39). In fact, the document provides a comprehensive description of evangelization as including "proclamation, witness, teaching, sacraments, love of neighbor: all of these aspects are the means by which the one Gospel is transmitted and they constitute the essential elements of evangelization itself" (GDC 46). Simply, evangelization is concurrent with the entire mission of the church, one that seeks to embody a life of love that transforms the temporal order; to bear persuasive witness to the way of life characteristic of Christianity; to initiate into Christian faith through catechesis, the sacraments, and maturation in Christian communal life; to foster communion among the faithful through the catechetical and sacramental ministries of the church; and to flame the desire for mission within the world (GDC 48). The stages of evangelization, as the document recognizes, are fluid and may include:

> missionary activity directed toward nonbelievers and those who live in religious indifference; initial catechetical activity for those who choose the Gospel and for those who need to complete or modify their initiation; pastoral activity directed toward the Christian faithful f mature faith in the bosom of the Christian community. (GDC 49)

Yet, the fundamental goal of evangelization is the same in each of the stages: the renewal of the human race, of culture, of all existence in light of the

Gospel, of a revelation that is proclaimed, celebrated, and lived through visible signs and deeds.

Catechesis, though not reducible to evangelization, is integral to each stage of evangelization, including first proclamation, Christian initiation, ongoing formation into faith, and Catholic schools. It seeks to promote a living encounter with Christ, one that opens one up to a participation in the triune life of God (GDC 98–99). The directory emphasizes the christocentric and trinitarian nature of all catechesis, even more so than *Catechesi Tradendae*. The Directory comments:

> Following the pedagogy of Jesus in revelation of the Father, of himself as the Son, and of the Holy Spirit, catechesis shows the most intimate life of God, starting with his salvific works for the good of humanity. The works of God reveal who he is and the mystery of his inner Being throws light on all of his works. It is analogous with human relationships: people reveal themselves by their actions and, the more deeply we know them, the better we understand what they do. (GDC 100)

This paragraph is important enough that it deserves further attention. The catechist contemplates salvation history precisely as manifesting the interior life of God. This act of contemplation results in a transformation of our own humanity—a realization of what it means to be human in light of the pedagogy of faith. Consider for a moment the fact that Jesus Christ, fully God and fully human, dies upon the cross and is then resurrected. When the catechist teaches this doctrine, immersing the student into the intricacies of salvation history, he or she is not simply proclaiming a historical fact. The catechist is inviting the student to participate in the life of God, in an act of contemplative learning; to perceive anew with wonder that the very root of all existence, the Creator of the world, has entered into the fullness of the human condition, offering himself in love unto the end. Nothing is more transformative, nothing more humanizing than such a doctrine.

And importantly in this act of teaching, of immersion into Christ's life as embodied in doctrine, we learn that to become divine is not to give up our humanity, to radically separate Christian life from life in general, precisely because it is the Word made flesh that offers our humanity, our history, our temporality as a gift to the Father. The document makes clear that "the human and social implications of the Christian concept of God are immense" (GDC 100). Recently, on the feast of the Ascension, Pope Francis preached regarding Christ:

He always forgives us, He is our advocate, He always defends us. We must never forget this. The Ascension of Jesus into heaven then reveals to us this reality that is so comforting for our journey: in Christ, true God and true man, our humanity was brought to God; He has opened the passage up for us, He is like a leader at the head of the rope when you scale a mountain, who has reached the summit and draws us up to Him, leading us to God. If we entrust our lives to Him, if we let ourselves be guided by Him we are sure to be in safe hands. In the hands of our Savior, our advocate.[11]

It is the humanity of Christ, visible in the wounds that still mark his resurrected and ascended body, which transfigures every facet of our existence into an offering of God. The couple that welcomes a newborn infant comes to know Christ ever more deeply, as their own sense of wonder, of exhaustion, of terror at being parents is offered up to the Father in love. The middle-aged man who receives a diagnosis of a terminal illness comes to know Christ as he gives himself over to the reality of the shortness of life, of physical relationships that come to an end. The marginalized, those who are ignored by church and society alike, enter into Christ's very life as they seek divine love even in the faces of those who mutilate their humanity. We gaze at Christ, we contemplate his humanity, precisely because in Christ we come to know that the only way to be human is not to grasp, to hang on at all costs, to consume until the last drop, but to give all of our existence away in love.

While the *General Directory for Catechesis* fundamentally deals with the catechetical ministry of the church, it also addresses (at least in a very partial manner), the relationship between liturgical prayer and evangelization. Liturgical homilies, the sacraments of Christian initiation, and eucharistic communion are all integral to the process of evangelization in the church (GDC 48). Yet, the document treats liturgical formation most fully when turning to an elucidation of the fundamental tasks of a catechesis centered in evangelization. Quoting the entire text that deals with the liturgical task of catechesis:

> Christ is always present in his Church, especially in "liturgical celebrations." Communion with Jesus Christ leads to the celebration of his salvific presence in the sacraments, especially in the Eucharist. The church ardently desires that all the Christian faithful be brought to that full, conscious, and active participation which is required by the very nature of the liturgy and the dignity of the baptismal priesthood. For this reason, catechesis, along with promoting a knowledge of

> the meaning of the liturgy and the sacraments, must also educate the disciples of Jesus Christ "for prayer, for thanksgiving, for repentance, for praying with confidence, for community spirit, for understanding correctly the meaning of the creeds," as all of this is necessary for a true liturgical life. (GDC 85)

Note that central to the liturgical task of catechesis is promotion of *full, conscious, and active participation*, intrinsic to the very nature of liturgy and the dignity of those who are baptized. The end of liturgical formation is nothing less than the creation within each Christian of a *habitus*, a disposition dedicated to living a liturgical life. In fact, the pedagogy of divine-human exchange, in which the wonders of that divine life in Christ are knit into the human life, are especially important since "in the liturgy, all personal life becomes a spiritual oblation" (GDC 87).

Thus, implicit in the document (although never fully developed) is the function of liturgical prayer within the broader contours of evangelization. If evangelization is the transformation of all human existence, all human culture, in light of the Gospel, then nothing is more important to the evangelical mission of the church then those liturgical rites that enable us to offer our humanity to the Father through the Son in the unity of the Spirit. Indeed, if one is to propose a critique of the church's recent documents on evangelization, these documents are not clear enough regarding the "evangelical" nature of the liturgy.

A Liturgical Theology of Evangelization: *Sacrosanctum Concilium*

When giving talks in parishes, dioceses, or universities on liturgical renewal in the church, I am often asked the following question: How can we increase full, conscious, and active participation in our parish? The pastor or liturgy director is drawing on one of the key ideas from the Constitution on the Sacred Liturgy, a phrase that the German liturgist Josef Jungmann called the refrain of the council.[12] Yet, I always have a hard time answering the question precisely because this document was not simply interested in rallying assemblies to sing with more vigor, to sign up liturgical ministers *en masse*, and to perform gestures with the appropriate level of dramatic flair. Instead, *Sacrosanctum Concilium* sought to foster a renewal of the entirety of Christian life, a deeper understanding of what it means to be the church pilgriming in the world: "From the very beginning the revival of the liturgy went hand in hand with the renewal of the concept of the Church. If such a picture of the Church is engrafted on the hearts of the faithful by rendering accessible to them such a liturgy, they will be much better equipped to act in the world as Christians." [13] Indeed, although the proper grammar was not available at the time the document was composed, *Sacrosanctum Concilium* situates the liturgical prayer of the church within the domain of evangelization as described above. While a wholesale treatment of the document is not possible, I want to focus on five features of this document relevant to evangelization: the location of liturgy within the broader narrative of salvation; the prominence of the paschal mystery in the text; the ecclesiological vision offered by the document; the claim of liturgy's function as glorifying God and sanctifying humanity through signs; and lastly, a closer examination of what is meant by full, conscious, and active participation.

Liturgy and Salvation History

Even a hasty reading of *Sacrosanctum Concilium* results in a rather stunning insight: a document on liturgy begins not with a discussion of liturgical ritual, of where the various liturgical actors should stand, or even of the history of liturgical prayer itself. The document commences with a vision of liturgy as a participation in salvation history: "For the liturgy, through which 'the work of our redemption takes place,' especially in the divine sacrifice of the Eucharist, is supremely effective in enabling the faithful to express in their lives and portray to others the mystery of Christ and the real nature of the true church" (SC 2).[14] Christian liturgy is not mere ceremony; it is not the production of rituals appropriate to specific settings. When someone proclaims that a University of Notre Dame football game is a liturgical event, such a person has missed the essence of Christian worship. In the liturgical rites of the church, each person participates in the salvific activity of the triune God, who has unfolded his love through the ages. The liturgy, as Cyprian Vagaggini notes, "is nothing else than a certain phase of revelation, a certain way in which the meaning of revelation is realized in us." [15]

That liturgical prayer is a participation in the unfolding of the narrative of salvation is a stunning claim. When my infant son was baptized, as the priest blessed the waters, as the acclamation of the assembly rained down upon him, as water was poured over his head, and the Father, the Son, and the Holy Spirit were invoked, he slept. In the midst of his sleep, he entered into the communion of the church, of those of us marked with the sign of the cross. His history, so short, is now part of that larger narrative whereby

God created the cosmos as an act of love; whereby he nurtured our ungrate-
ful hearts through the tender mercy he bestowed upon Abraham, Isaac, and
Jacob; whereby he saved his people from the slavery of Egypt, softening
their hardened hearts as he pilgrimed with Israel through the barrenness of
a desert he restored to life through manna from above; whereby in the fullness of time, God sent his only Son to reveal to us that power and prestige
are but shadows compared to the reality of a life of total, self-giving love.
The narrative of salvation, continually unfolding in the liturgical rites of
the church, becomes our own through participation in the liturgy. My son's
entire life, his eating and sleeping and gazing with total wonder upon every
source of light, is fertile ground for the enfleshment of the Word.

　　Thus, redemption is not simply an intellectual possibility for the Christian. As Yves Congar comments, the salutary quality to liturgical prayer
"is not only taught to us or merely brought to our notice; it is celebrated,
realized, rendered present and communicated, not simply as a doctrine or
truth, but as a reality." [16] Liturgy is a privileged performance of evangelization, one in which our humanity comes to experience the reality of God
through visible signs.

Liturgy and the Paschal Mystery

　　In fact, the document as it moves forward says even more about our participation in salvation history through liturgical prayer. There is, perhaps, no
more important concept in the document than that of the paschal mystery,
mentioned for the first time in article 6 of *Sacrosanctum Concilium*.[17] What
is meant by the term paschal mystery? Quoting Jungmann:

> The term *paschale mysterium* describes . . . the expression "mystery
> of Christ" . . . the real kernel of the Christian order of salvation: the
> act with which Christ has redeemed us and which is continued in the
> saving activity of the Church. Like the *pascha* of the Old Testament,
> it is a remembrance of God's redeeming acts of salvation, the presence
> of salvation and the promise of the consummating future. It underlines
> at the same time the basic triumphant Easter character, which is of
> the essence of Christianity, of the work of the Church, its message
> and salvation.[18]

Importantly, the term is not new but is drawn from Odo Casel's *The Mystery
of Christian Worship* (1932).[19] A closer reading of this text enables one to
see that the paschal mystery is not only shorthand for describing the death

and resurrection of Christ; but instead it is a term essential to grasping the evangelical function of the liturgy.

Casel's work, albeit integral to the development of the liturgical movement, is in reality a response to a disillusionment of the religious imagination. At the beginning of the text, he writes:

> It is usual nowadays to talk a great deal about the brotherhood of nations and service to humanity; but behind all this there is not that deeper love which is a sharing in the very love of God himself, his *agape*, but instead the self-divinization of mankind, which sees in itself the god it means to worship. Community means nothing except individuals lumped in a mass, joined together for the sole purpose of fighting off, by their collective weight, any power which might make a claim to rule over them: a spectacle of brute power.[20]

All of life, according to Casel, has become disenchanted. We view the world as subatomic particles and governmental power grabs. At the same time, religion can easily be reduced to a series of dogmatic propositions, on one hand, or "a more or less emotionally toned attitude towards 'The divine,' which binds itself to no dogmatic or moral system whatever," on the other.[21] But Christianity is not a religion in either of these senses. Christianity is a "mystery," "a deed of God's, the execution of an everlasting plan of his through an act which proceeds from his eternity, realized in time and the world, and returning once more to him its goal in eternity." [22] Through the mystery of Christianity, humanity is invited to return to the Father, back to the totality of divine love that was our origin before the fall.

The fullness of this mystery is revealed in Christ, specifically in his sacrifice upon the cross. Casel writes:

> At the mid-point of the Christian religion . . . stands the sacred *Pasch*, the passage which the Son of God who appeared in the flesh of sin, makes to the Father. The pasch is a sacrifice with the consecration of the person that flows from it; it is the sacrifice of the God-man in death on the cross, and his resurrection to glory: it is the Church's sacrifice in communion with and by the power of the crucified God-man, and the wonderful joining to God, the divinization which is its effect.[23]

The sacrifice of divine love, revealed in Christ's self-gift upon the cross, is that very same sacrifice that the church enacts in her rites, in her liturgical worship.[24] And as the humanity of Christ—embodied in the church—offers this worship together with the Son, then our very humanity is made divine:

"the time from the ascension to the parousia has this meaning: to reproduce in individuals the fact of Christ, the mystery of Christ, to enter into his mystery, to be absorbed by it." [25]

Often, the problem with such theological claims is that they are difficult to see when one moves to the level of the concrete, the particular. I have attended a slew of eucharistic liturgies in which rather than "divinized," I have been sent forth dumbed, dulled, and disordered. But for a moment, consider a Sunday assembly and the sheer range of human affections, desires, and narratives included there. A widow enters the sanctuary, devastated by the loss of her husband. A soon-to-be high school graduate is overjoyed by news that he has been accepted to the university of his dreams. Many couples enter this assembly worried about the burden of bills and the fearful possibility of losing a job. When the eucharistic prayer is offered, these joys and desires, these sorrows and disappointments become part of that sacrifice of praise offered by the priest and assembly alike. Our entire selves are joined to Christ's sacrifice to the Father, as we give ourselves away in prayer in response to the God who first loved us. And if we recognize what our humanity has become through this prayer, if we can see that every aspect of ourselves is part of this gift, then we come to know our responsibility to offer that return-gift of love to the neighbor: "Here we can see the full human import of the radical newness brought by Christ in the Eucharist: the worship of God in our lives cannot be relegated to something private and individual, but tends by its nature to permeate every aspect of our existence." [26]

Thus, the very nature of the paschal mystery is that which draws us out of ourselves, returning us to the love of Father revealed in Christ, a love inspired by the Spirit that seeks to echo throughout the cosmos and history alike. The paschal mystery is, for this reason, more than shorthand for the death and resurrection of Christ. It is the pedagogy of the liturgy in which our humanity is lifted up to the Father through Christ. The paschal mystery, celebrated in the liturgy, is at the heart of every act of evangelization.

Liturgy and the Church

Although *Sacrosanctum Concilium* is often treated for its liturgical vision, it has recently been argued that it is the preeminent ecclesiological document, pertaining to the very nature of the Church. [27] How so? Quoting the text:

the church is both human and divine, visible but endowed with invisible realities, zealous in action and dedicated to contemplation, present in the world, yet a migrant, so constituted that in it the human is directed toward and subordinated to the divine, the visible to the invisible, action to contemplation, and this present world to that city yet to come, the object of our quest (see Heb 13:14). The liturgy daily builds up those who are in the church, making of them a holy temple of the Lord, a dwelling-place for God in the Spirit (see Eph 2:21-22), to the mature measure of the fullness of Christ (see Eph 4:13). (SC 2)

The church is not a bureaucracy, a sociological entity alone. In the church's actions, it is the invisible Christ and his Spirit who works through visible means. The church offers the liturgy in conjunction with the sacrifice of Christ, thus participating in Christ's self-gift upon the cross. Words are spoken, hymns are sung, prayers are chanted, human affections are raised to the living God, and in each case, they are accepted by the Father through the sacrifice of Christ the mediator.

It should be noticed that the document at no point presents the celebration of the liturgy as the sole responsibility of the priest. Instead, "liturgical services have to do with the whole body, the church. They make it visible and have effects on it. But they also touch individual members of the church in different ways, depending on ranks, roles and levels of participation" (SC 26). The church, after Christ the liturgist, is the principal liturgical actor.[28] And the rites of the church are not the private affairs of prelates or liturgical committees but celebrations of the Body of the church, which visibly, audibly, and tangibly manifest the identity of the church as a sacrament of unity (SC 26).

In fact, the liturgy is the most sacred of the church's activity, not because everything else the church does is peripheral to the formation of disciples, but because

> the liturgy is the summit toward which the activity of the church is directed; it is also the source from which all its power flows. For the goal of apostolic endeavor is that all who are made children of God by faith and Baptism should come together to praise God in the midst of his church, to take part in the sacrifice and to eat the Lord's Supper. (SC 10)

There is a kind of strangeness to this claim. As the fathers of the Second Vatican Council noticed about this passage, is not the ultimate end of the

Christian life love, peace, unity of will?[29] Is the goal of apostolic endeavor really liturgy? Of course, as the reader would recognize by now, these questions in fact reflect a false dichotomy. The liturgy of the church sacramentally expresses, through visible signs, that unity of love that all of humanity is called to through Jesus Christ.

Again, rather than remain at the level of theological abstraction, it may be useful to turn to the concrete. In the context of present-day American life, there are numerous ways that we are unified, becoming one in a common mission or purpose—sometimes against our wills. Attending an NFL game, for example, is a unifying experience, one in which the pulsating music, the chants of the crowd, the joyance of reveling in a violent hit or a brilliant pass from a franchise quarterback gathers a stadium of strangers together in a common purpose. Of course, such unity is not peaceful; it is a form of self-worship whereby a city or community delights in its accomplishments, in its own glories, in its own self-worth (implicitly against the "other guys"). Christian liturgy is distinct from this. It is not a violent, forced gathering of those marked by the sign of the cross. It is not a form of self-worship, whereby we praise God for choosing a people as worthy as us. Liturgical prayer reveals an ecclesiology of gift, of gratitude,[30] whereby the Body of Christ, the People of God, the Temple of the Holy Spirit is unified, not by its own efforts, by the folly of force, but by the pacifistic gift of a God who loved unto the end. As Joseph Ratzinger writes:

> Only a power and love that is stronger than all of our own initiatives can build up a fruitful and reliable community and impart to it the impetus of a fruitful mission. The unity of the Church, which is founded upon the love of the one Lord, does not destroy what is particular in the individual communities; rather, it builds them up and holds them together as a real communion with the Lord and with each other. The love of Christ, which is present for all ages in the Sacrament of his Body, awakens our love and heals our love: the Eucharist is the foundation of community as it is of mission, day by day.[31]

Liturgical prayer, exemplified in the eucharistic liturgy, is the summit and font of ecclesial identity because in this prayer, we are slowly made one by the love of Christ, a divine love that heals our disordered affections. Such a love does not erase difference; it is not a banal unity of the same. Yet, the church's liturgical worship does reveal the destiny of all humanity whereby we will be made whole, one, a single gift of love offered to the Father "integrated by the Spirit of the Lord into the communion in which the totality of what is human—with its differences, its diversity, its joys, and its sorrows—has become one with Christ Jesus in the *agape* of the cross and resurrection." [32]

Thus, the church's liturgy is a matter of evangelization because it both signifies and makes real that unity of love, of self-gift, which is the destiny of all of humanity in Christ. The church emerges forth from its act of worship, its members enlightened by communion with the Lord, seeking to offer this gift of self to each person they encounter. A gift of love that is not controlling, that does not reduce difference to a facile unity. Such love, such gift of self to the world seeks a unity made possible only in the love of God poured up generously in the liturgical rites of the church. A church that does recognize its evangelical mission to the world has not yet grasped the depths of love manifested in its worship.

The Glorification of God and the Sanctification of Humanity through Signs

Thus far we have treated the theological—and, as it turns out, evangelical—foundations of *Sacrosanctum Concilium*. Liturgical prayer is a participation in salvation history, the offering of every facet of our humanity to the Father as an act of love, one that results in our passage through Christ to divine life. Such prayer is not simply individualistic but seeks to unify all of humanity into a single sacrifice of love to the Father, embodied in the divine-human life of the church. Yet how do the liturgical rites of the church make this possible? How is a particular individual, who attends the liturgy, inspired to such self-giving love? *Sacrosanctum Concilium* clarifies this point. Quoting the text:

> The liturgy, then, is rightly seen as an exercise of the priestly office of Jesus Christ. In the liturgy the sanctification of women and men is given expression in symbols perceptible [*signa sensibilia*] by the senses and is carried out in ways appropriate to each of them. In it, complete and definitive public worship is performed by the mystical body of Jesus Christ, that is, by the Head and his members. (SC 7)

This paragraph of *Sacrosanctum Concilium* requires closer attention, precisely because the text includes a key insight into the pedagogy of liturgical prayer. In fact, two functions of liturgy (the glorification of God and the sanctification of women and men) are united together through the concept of "symbols" or perhaps a better translation "sensible signs" (*signa sensibilia*).

For the sake of clarifying the function of liturgy in the church's mission of evangelization, it will be important to grasp the theological import of the term "sensible signs," as well as how these signs enable humanity to glorify God and to enter into a process of sanctification.

Why is there an emphasis in the passage on sensible signs? Commenting on liturgy as a complex of sensible signs, Cyprian Vagaggini writes:

> under the veil of the sign, of any sign, the reality of the thing signi-fied is reached, and that the reality reaches us through this sensible veil because there is a certain real, though partial, identity between the sign and the reality signified. We must understand that the sign is the bridge over which our encounter is made with the invisible reality and this reality is made present to us, even if that encounter and that presence are always very imperfect because the sign can never contain and transmit all the wealth of the invisible reality which is expressed in it. Only if we have a lively sense of all this are we predisposed for entering the world of the liturgy.[33]

Sacrosanctum Concilium takes this insight, drawn from sacramental theology, and applies it to the liturgy as a whole. Liturgical prayer consists of a myriad of sacred signs, all of which refer to the reality of divine love manifested in Christ and now communicated through the church. For example, consider the assembly. The gathering of the people of God for divine worship is not akin to a club, who decides it would be helpful for the sake of group cohesion to meet at least once a week. Rather, "for one who knows how to see through the veil of the sign, it is a convocation, an *ekklesia*, of God in Christ Jesus, an assembling 'in the name' of Christ."[34] Liturgy includes a host of such signs ranging from speech, gestures, elements and objects, liturgical art, and persons.[35]

Importantly, this pedagogy of signification operates on a variety of levels. According to Vagaggini, signs have four dimensions: they are demonstrative, obligating, commemorative, and prophetic.[36] The demonstrative dimension of a sign points toward invisible, sacred realities—those theological foundations of the liturgy described above.[37] A stained glass window, depicting Catherine of Siena, is a demonstrative sign insofar as the light that illumines the colored glass produces within us a delirious delight, an elevating of our imaginations for a moment to consider the God who is the light seeking to illuminate every member of the assembly into a luminous icon of sanctity. Yet, every sign is also obligating, a moral sign remanding a new way of being in light of our interaction with the sign.[38] Continuing with the example of a stained glass window, the Christian who perceives the beauty of God's own light cannot remain complacent, pleased with his or her enjoyment of the window. Instead, the Christian must ask oneself, am I an effective medium for allowing the light of divine love to manifest itself even now? Do I perceive in my neighbor a visible sign of God's own light? Further, every sign in liturgy is commemorative, pointing toward that narrative of salvation fully revealed in Christ but already operative since the time of Adam.[39] Again, the stained glass window brings the entire assembly back to the moment of creation in which light first illuminated the chaos, while also presenting to the assembly an image of St. Catherine who has become a mirror for us seeking to contemplate God's own light spilling out into history. Lastly, liturgical signs are prophetic, pointing toward "heavenly glory and of the worship in the future Jerusalem." [40] Our example of a stained glass window is once again an apt one. For in our contemplation of a church bathed in the refracted light of these windows, we glimpse momentarily the very essence of the God who is for us the light that knows no darkness.

This four-fold signification is essential to grasping how the liturgy sanctifies humanity, how it glorifies God. Again quoting Vagaggini:

> In the concrete liturgical reality, the action of God who sanctifies and the response of the Church who renders her worship to God are closely intertwined and cannot in fact be separated, being like two correlative and indivisible aspects of one and the same reality. The ultimate reason for this is the intimate copenetration of the divine action and the human response in the work of man's sanctification and of worship.[41]

Every liturgical action of the church is the concrete, incarnational, and sacramental manner in which God bestows to humanity grace upon grace, gift upon gift. The concrete, bodily signs of the liturgy enable humanity to participate in God's own life as our imaginations, our desires, every facet of our being is infused with sanctifying grace. Simultaneously, the liturgy of the church is a proper glorification of the living God, the church carrying out that most just action of adoration. The church does not glorify God abstractly, as disembodied souls who like to think pleasing thoughts about the triune God. As the church carries out its duty of worship through sacred signs, signs that form and renew our imaginations, we are sanctified, divinized, returned to our vocation as creatures made in the image and likeness of God.[42]

What does this have to do with evangelization? Simply, the use of sacred signs to glorify God in liturgical prayer and sanctify humanity is already an act of evangelization. Our voices, our artistic creations, our affections and desires are knit into the unfolding plan of divine love as we ourselves partici-pate in worship. We become worshippers, adorers of the living God, capable of participating in God's own life. The signs that we engage with in liturgical worship are to incarnate themselves into every part of our lives, not simply individually but as a social group. Members of the Body of Christ, the visible church, must seek to become all that we receive in worship. By no means is this sanctification automatic, magical, or immediate. As *Sacrosanctum Concilium* makes clear, "in order that the liturgy may be able to produce its full effects it is necessary that the faithful come to it with proper dispositions, that their minds be attuned to their voices, and that they cooperate with heavenly grace lest they receive it in vain" (SC 11). But to the community that gives itself over to the liturgical rites of the church with such dispositions, liturgical prayer is that pedagogy of God whereby every facet of culture, every aspect of society, every individual body and desire is lifted up in love to the Father through immersion into sacred signs that glorify and sanctify.[43]

Full, Conscious, and Active Participation

Having considered the theological foundations and pedagogical prin-ciples of liturgical prayer, we may now return to that famous refrain of the Second Vatican Council:

> It is very much the wish of the church that all the faithful should be led to take that full, conscious, and active part in liturgical celebrations which is demanded by the very nature of the liturgy, and to which the Christian people "a chosen race, a royal priesthood, a holy nation, a redeemed people" (1 Pet 2:9, 4-5) have a right and to which they are bound by reason of their baptism. (SC 14)

By now, it should be obvious that full, conscious, and active participation is not simply encouraging parishes to a frenetic, external performance of rites. It does not mean that everyone in the parish is constantly performing gestures, speaking, singing, and making noise. Rather, this participation includes immersion of our imaginations, our very bodies, into the salvation history that liturgical prayer unfolds; it is a participation that culminates in our being taken up into the paschal mystery of Christ, one in which as we give our humanity over to the Father, we become divine; it is a participation in the church, a community that finds its source not in its own ideas, its own theories, but in the efficacious love of God healing the wounded heart of individual and society alike; it is a participation in sacred signs, which serve as concrete ways that our humanity slowly practices the art of self-giving love through the glorification of God. For this reason, full, conscious, and active participation is necessarily external and internal, the speaking of concrete words that lead us to contemplate and become that love of God for the salvation of the world.

It is perhaps for this reason that I have such a difficult time advocating "best practices" for parishes to promote full, conscious, and active participation. It is not simply a matter of increasing external activity, offering guides for what the various symbols of worship mean, of improving microphone systems, or finding the right music that everyone can sing. These are important facets of liturgical worship. But it is not enough. As Joseph Ratzinger writes:

> True liturgical education cannot consist in learning and experimenting with external activities. Instead one must be led toward the essential *actio* that makes the liturgy what it is, toward the transforming power of God, who wants, through what happens in the liturgy, to transform us and the world.[44]

The Christian faithful must slowly learn, through the art of self-giving love made possible through the mystery of the liturgy, to allow external participation (the speaking of words, the participation in a procession, the singing of a hymn) to become an internal gift of self to God and neighbor alike.[45] To really mean what it is that we pray; to bring the sacrifice of our lives to the altar as a eucharistic offering of love; to mark ourselves with the sign of the cross no longer in a perfunctory way but as a commitment that our body might become an icon of Christ's own self-gift for the world.

The externals are essential. Liturgical participation cannot be reduced solely to silent contemplation if this deeper internal participation is to be made possible. Signs matter, and for this reason, the remainder of *Sacrosanctum Concilium* is taken up with a reform of the liturgy "in order that the Christian people may be more certain to derive an abundance of graces from it" (SC 21). But the promotion of full, conscious, and active participation cannot simply focus on externals. It must foster within the Christian the proper dispositions to participate in liturgical prayer in a way that results in a transformation of each individual, of the history of humanity, of the cosmos itself. In this way, the promotion of full, conscious, and active participation in liturgical prayer is nothing less than a privileged way of evangelizing.

In this chapter, I offered a liturgical theology within the domain of the church's understanding of evangelization. I first defined evangelization as the transformation of humanity through the particulars of the Gospel. Evangelization is not a sectarian or violent persuasion of others to join the church. Instead, it is an imaginative activity in which the church proposes a vision of what humanity can become when we give ourselves over to the prodigal love of the triune God. Evangelization is the very mission of the church, and it has been defined most fully in documents that treat catechesis.

In the second part of this chapter, I turned to the liturgical theology inscribed in *Sacrosanctum Concilium* to discover a robust understanding of how liturgy is itself integral to evangelization. Liturgical prayer invites the faithful to knit their own narrative into salvation history; to participate in the paschal mystery of Christ; to become a sacrament of unity through the church—one that serves as an icon of peace for all the world; to become sanctified and divinized through the glorification of God through sensible and sacred signs. Full, conscious, and active participation in the sensible signs of liturgical prayer results in the re-creation of our desires, our imaginations, and ultimately our very will. Every facet of our humanity (both individually and socially) is elevated to divine life, and we emerge forth from such prayer committed to the transformation of the world, having become practiced in the art of self-giving love.

Thus, liturgical prayer is integral to the church's mission of evangelization. The promotion of full, conscious, and active participation is pivotal to the ongoing mission of evangelization. Yet in the last several years, a new term has entered into ecclesial parlance: "the new evangelization." It is to the treatment of this term that I now devote my attention.

The New Evangelization
Liturgical Secularity

2

Liturgical prayer, as the last chapter noted, is intrinsic to the mission of evangelization. Our engagement in the church's liturgy transforms our affections, our desires, and every facet of our lives offered out of the depths of love to the Father. Yet, a further question awaits the careful inquirer: why must this evangelization become new? Was there something stale about the previous articulation of evangelization?

The present chapter seeks to explore this question in two parts. In the first section, I define the new evangelization as a process of spiritual renewal of the church, one that includes a close attention to the present-day context. That is, the new evangelization is not so much a marginalizing of previous conceptions of what constitutes evangelization. It is not a retrograde movement, which seeks to "dial back" the reforms of the Second Vatican Council. Instead, it is a spiritual renewal that recognizes that all those who come to perceive the persuasive beauty of the claims of Christian faith will become evangelists. Thus, the new evangelization depends upon a return to pedagogy of the basics, a return to the sources whereby we seek to understand the rich insights at the heart of Christian doctrine and practice for being human in the modern world.

In the second, I offer a diagnosis of the context in which new evangelization takes places, what I call an American form of secularization. This portion of the chapter draws upon the sociological research of Christian Smith with particular attention to his findings relative to adolescent and emerging adult religious life. According to Smith, American religious life is characterized by what he comes to call "Moralistic Therapeutic Deism," a quasi-faith incommensurate with the substantive claims of how God acts in history within Christianity. In the third portion of the chapter, I draw out the liturgical and catechetical implications regarding this parasitic approach to religious understanding, which has an implicit secularizing influence upon the theological imagination. American secularization is a thinning of the theological imagination, a loss of desire for mystagogy, and an almost exclusive focus upon individual flourishing. These three features of American religious life have an effect upon the formative nature of the liturgical life of the church. Yet, this process of internal secularization can be healed most effectively through a renewed attention to liturgical strategies that reinvigorate each member of the church for the fruitful practice of such prayer.

What Is the New Evangelization?

When entering into conversations with diocesan leaders committed to the new evangelization, I frequently ask them what they mean by the term. In the myriad of conversations that I have had with such leaders, I rarely encounter a consistent answer. For some, the new evangelization seeks to actively dispose the technological resources of the modern world to proclaim the Gospel (for this reason, it is the work of the younger generation). For others, the novelty of this evangelization pertains to a deeper commitment to catechetical formation, a pedagogy of the basics often neglected since the council. More often, I encounter a benign bemusement regarding the term—a recognition among pastoral ministers, both priests and laity alike, that bishops believe the new evangelization to be integral to the work of the church but an awareness that the term molds itself to whatever pastoral goals that specific bishop seeks to accomplish within his diocese.

Despite the sometimes expansive use of the term among clergy and laity, the new evangelization of the church has a decided meaning. Historically, the new evangelization (as used by John Paul II) sought to respond to the reality that many baptized Catholics, especially in the Western world, have received the sacraments of initiation but for the most part are not formed in the practice of faith. As John Paul II writes in *Redemptoris Missio* (RM):

> there is an intermediate situation, particularly in countries with ancient Christian roots, and occasionally in the younger Churches as well, where entire groups of the baptized have lost a living sense of the faith, or even no longer consider themselves members of the Church, and live a life far removed from Christ and his Gospel. In this case what is needed is a "new evangelization" or a "re-evangelization." [1]

Yet, the very same document also refers to a time of new evangelization, which includes a spiritual recommitment of the entire church to the public embodiment of the Gospel in the world (RM 3). Nascent in *Redemptoris*

Missio is a larger sense of a spiritual renewal, a recultivation of the imagination of the entire church.

Although John Paul II provided the impetus for the new evangelization, Benedict XVI's pontificate was particularly dedicated to concretizing this term through theological inquiry.[2] In Benedict XVI's two substantive apostolic exhortations, *Sacramentum Caritatis* and *Verbum Domini* (VD), the theme of the new evangelization looms large. The Eucharist is evangelizing for Benedict XVI, precisely because it becomes a source of renewal for the individual, who begins to perceive the world eucharistically through seeing how all facets of human culture might express the logic of love at the heart of the eucharistic gift (*Sacramentum Caritatis* 77–78). Likewise, Benedict XVI emphasizes that the new evangelization includes a persuasive proclamation of the Word of God, one that commits the church to the mission of proclaiming divine love.[3] A careful reading of Benedict's apostolic exhortations reveals an imaginative theological vision, a catechetical theology that is persuasive and fundamental. For Benedict XVI, the new evangelization includes a returning to the sources of Christian faith not in an antiquarian manner but as a way of rousing the Christian to the logic of self-giving love in the public sphere. For example, in teaching anew the doctrine of transubstantiation in a scientific age, he writes in *Sacramentum Caritatis*:

> The substantial conversion of bread and wine into his body and blood introduces within creation the principle of a radical change, a sort of "nuclear fission," to use an image familiar to us today, which penetrates to the heart of all being, a change meant to set off a process which transforms reality, a process leading ultimately to the transfiguration of the entire world, to the point where God will be all in all (cf. 1 Cor 15:28). (*Sacramentum Caritatis* 11)

An astute reader will note that Benedict draws on a scientific image in his explication of this traditional Catholic doctrine, while also describing transubstantiation as ordered, not to a bizarre magical change of bread into Body and Blood, but the very transformation of the cosmos through love. The theological implication of this pedagogy, relative to the new evangelization, is that Christian teaching must become imaginative, a discourse that is true, good, and beautiful. It must use imagery familiar to the contemporary person, not in explaining away the mystery of Christian faith, but as a way of drawing humanity deeper into the divine plan of salvation carried out in Christ. Thus for Benedict XVI, the new evangelization takes on a certain style, a way of retrieving the heart of Christian teaching and proclaiming it through a truthful rhetoric of love.

This commitment to the new evangelization as a spiritual renewal of the church is articulated most clearly in the *Lineamenta* leading up to the Synod of the New Evangelization, which took place in October 2012. Fundamentally, as the document makes clear, the new evangelization is nothing less than:

> renewed spiritual efforts in the life of faith within the local Churches, starting with a process to discern the changes in various cultural and social settings and their impact on Christian life, to reread the memory of faith and to undertake new responsibilities and generate new energies to joyously and convincingly proclaim the Gospel of Jesus Christ. (*Lineamenta* 5)

Importantly, the new evangelization is not about bunkering down with our fellow sectarians and condemning the world to hell. Nor for that matter is it assuming a dour face, getting serious about religion, and in the meantime denying the very Good News that Christ has conquered death and sin through the instrument of *our* humanity. Instead, the new evangelization is:

> synonymous with mission, requiring the capacity to set out anew, go beyond boundaries and broaden horizons. The new evangelization is the opposite of self-sufficiency, a withdrawal into oneself, a *status quo* mentality and an idea that pastoral programmes are simply to proceed as they did in the past . . . [it] is the time for the Church to call upon every Christian community to evaluate their pastoral practice on the basis of the missionary character of their programmes and activities. (*Lineamenta* 10)

Therefore, in the case of the parish, the new evangelization requires a discernment of how deeply the Word of God echoes within us; how splendidly our liturgical celebrations effect a renewed communion with God and one another; and, how we manifest through mission the depths of love made possible through the contemplation of the Word of God and reception of the Body and Blood of Christ.

Still, the new evangelization offers a realistic approach to the proclamation of the Gospel. It gazes with sobriety upon the fields of culture, society, social communications, the economy, science and technology, as well as civic life (*Lineamenta* 6). One cannot help but notice that these arenas, though offering certain possibilities for the Gospel, also exhibit either a benign tedium or hostility toward the practice of faith. A church, dedicated to the mission of the new evangelization, seeks to form women and men who "know how to speak in ways that are intelligible to our times and proclaim, inside these arenas, the reasons for our hope which bolsters our witness" (cf. 1 Pet 3:15) (*Lineamenta* 22). The "newness" of the new evangelization is then not its object: rather it is to facilitate an encounter with Christ, one transformative of our humanity (*Lineamenta* 11). The new evangelization seeks to create disciples dedicated to the art of self-gift, to proclaiming the reality of Christ in a language that answers the deepest desires of human hope. The church's catechetical and liturgical life, its organization as parish, and its commitment to concrete practices of love in the world must all be renewed through the lens of this missionary zeal.

Liturgical prayer, as the subsequent chapters will argue, has a pivotal theological and spiritual function to fulfill in fostering this new evangelization. Yet, before turning to liturgy as a strategy for the church's renewal of mission, one must first treat the setting of this field of evangelization within the United States. In some sense, an additional book would be required to carry out this larger task. But in light of the theme of this book, let us focus on one fundamental aspect of cultural life, explicitly mentioned by the *Lineamenta*: secularization.

The Malaise of American Secularization

A cursory overview of the catechetical documents of the church in recent years leads the reader to the following conclusion: namely, in the present context, secularization is the primary obstacle to a fruitful appropriation of Christianity in the West. Yet, what do these documents mean by secularization? In the *General Directory for Catechesis* (GDC), secularization is treated as a manifestation of atheism, "which consists in an excessively autonomous view of man and of the world according to which it is entirely self-explanatory without any reference to God" (GDC 22). More recently, in the *Lineamenta*, it is perceived more broadly. No longer understood as

> a direct, outright denial of God, religion or Christianity . . . the secularizing movement has taken a more subtle tone in cultural forms which invade people's everyday lives and foster a mentality in which God is completely or partially left out of life and human consciousness. In this way, secularism has entered the Christian life and ecclesial communities and has become not simply an external threat for believers but something to be faced each day in life in the various manifestations of the so-called culture of relativism. (*Lineamenta* 6)

This less explicit form of secularization manifests itself through both a culture of individualism and consumerism, ideologies that the *National Directory for Catechesis* (NDC) notes "tends to trivialize, marginalize, or privatize the practice of religious faith."[4] Secularization is treated as the marginalization of religion from the rest of human life, including both human reason and the public sphere, caused by certain features of modern thought and life.[5]

One problem with this expansive depiction of secularity is that the precise nature of the problem is passed over at the expense of a diagnosis that equates consumerism, individualism, and atheism with secularization. Indeed, both consumerism and individualism may be symptoms of secularity, but they are not necessarily the defining feature of secularity. Nor should one conclude that modern "ideologies" are a direct cause of secularization.[6] Even further, some insights made possible by modern thought and social structures, such as the freedom of the individual, *could* lead to a more robust Christian identity rather than a weakened one, and thus serve as an inoculation against radical secularity.[7]

Of course, in making this claim, I am not suggesting that secularization is purely a sociological myth. Rather, like Charles Taylor, I recognize that the best way of defining the process is neither political (the disappearance of religious influence upon the state) nor psychological (the disappearance of religion from human consciousness) but "a move from a society where belief in God is unchallenged and indeed, unproblematic, to one in which it is understood to be one option among others, and frequently not the easiest to embrace."[8] Secularity, then, as Taylor notes, "is a matter of the whole context of understanding in which our moral, spiritual or religious experience and search takes place."[9] And thus reducing it to a series of influential ideas or unavoidable historical processes cannot explain the complex nature of secularization for religious belief in all contexts. The United States, despite high religious attendance vis-à-vis Europe, may be deeply influenced by secularity—a claim that is demonstrable only by attending to the specific religious narrative operative within an American context.

Thus, as Christian Smith has noted, a sociological analysis of the process of secularization requires "identifying and becoming highly familiar with the inherent and interactive operations and tendencies of all of the important causal mechanisms existing in modern social structures and practices that influence the strength and character of religion."[10] Ideas, apart from specific practices, do not lead to any social phenomenon since human beings are actors within the world, capable of choosing one way of life over another.[11] Secularization—in the United States, for example—was not an inescapable result of modernization, but instead a series of historical events in which specific persons successfully argued for a marginalization of religion from public life.[12] Likewise, those analyzing secularization theory have come to see that the processes of modernization do not function the same way across cultures, and thus no narrative of secularization looks exactly like others.[13] To diagnose and offer a treatment for secularization requires first an analysis of the nature of secularization within a specific context, as well as determining how structures and practices within a culture influence religious practice and understanding today. An account of secularization is best performed not through focusing upon –*isms* (consumerism, individualism, techno-centrism, relativism, pluralism, etc.) but the particularities of religious practice and understanding in a specific time and place.

One way of describing these conditions of belief is through attending to the results of Christian Smith's analysis of the National Study of Youth and Religion (NSYR). This survey, first conducted from July of 2002 to March of 2003, is in its third wave with its most recent interviews occurring in 2007 and 2008. The results of this longitudinal study, thus far covering the religious lives of American youth from ages fifteen to twenty-three, have been published in two studies, *Soul Searching: The Religious and Spiritual Lives of American Teenagers* (2005) and *Souls in Transition: The Religious and Spiritual Lives of Emerging Adults* (2009). The interviewees, chosen in the first stage, "were sampled to capture a broad range of difference among U.S. teens in religion, age, race, sex, socioeconomic status, rural-suburban residence, region of the country, and language spoken (English or Spanish)."[14] The third stage continued to represent the diversity of both American religion and culture, and thus, this study serves as an accurate lens of assessing American religiosity among youth cross-culturally.[15]

Nonetheless, one may challenge the wisdom of narrating American religious belief and practice through both adolescents and emerging adults.[16] As Smith himself concludes in comparing the results of the NSYR's third wave to the General Social Survey's data on religion collected between 1990 and 2006,[17] "one can be confident that whatever the remaining chapters reveal about the religious and spiritual lives of contemporary emerging adults, these persons are not typical religiously of all adults of all age groups in the United States."[18] On the other hand, young people, whether adolescents or emerging adults, do not learn religious beliefs or practices in a social vacuum. One of the more remarkable findings of the NSYR is the influence of parental and adult religious belief and practice upon adolescent and emerging adult religiosity. For example, among adolescents about three of every four say they have similar beliefs to their parents[19] and few explore religious traditions distinct from whatever was practiced within the home.[20] In fact, the strongest indicator of adolescent religiosity is parent religiosity.[21] Thus, adolescent and emerging adult religious belief, while distinct because of the life stage and historical period in which it is nurtured, is not incommensurate with assessments of adult faith. Finally, one should note that although adolescents and emerging adults are in different life stages than older adults, they do not necessarily reside in distinct social and cultural realities from one another. As Smith describes in his work, *What Is a Person?*, "institutional facts of social reality come into being, take on real ontological existence, and thus come to possess casual capacities to make events happen in the world."[22] Therefore, religious belief of adolescents and emerging adults are dependent upon definite historical and social facts that while "experienced" differently by younger generations are part of the world of adult religion nonetheless. As Smith addresses in both of his studies on religion among adolescents and emerging adults:

> studying the lives of young people in social context is a great way to enrich adults' perspective on their own adult society and lives. By examining the world of contemporary emerging adults . . . we hold up a mirror that reflects back to adults a telling picture of the larger adult world—their own world—into which emerging adults are moving.[23]

Hence, Smith's analysis of adolescent and emerging adult religious life offers us a window into the nature of American secularization, one essential to suggesting liturgical strategies for the new evangelization.

What can be said from Smith's analysis regarding American secularization? Importantly, secularization in the United States is not a matter of the disappearance of religion from human consciousness. Strikingly, both *Soul Searching* and *Souls in Transition* present young people with highly conventional religious beliefs. Adolescents who call themselves nonreligious are few, roughly only 16 percent of those surveyed.[24] Further, among the nonreligious, only 16 percent are either atheist or agnostic.[25] By the time these teens reach emerging adulthood, the nonreligious population has increased but by no means substantially so. Twenty-four percent of emerging adults call themselves nonreligious.[26] And again, of these 24 percent, only 17 percent do not believe in God.[27] As Smith and Snell write comparing the results of waves one/two and wave three of the data:

The majority of emerging adults also still are theists, believe that God rather than purely natural forces created the world, and identify with a more traditional view of the nature of God, Jesus Christ, divine judgment, angels, evil spirits, miracles, and life after death. Furthermore, most emerging adults seem positive about organized or mainstream religion in the United States. Most have respect for, are positive about, and are not personally turned off by it. The vast majority also have positive feelings about the religious tradition in which they were personally raised.[28]

Of course, one should not determine from this data that religion is an essential part of the lives of emerging adults, or that when adolescents and emerging adults use religious terms they do so in a "traditional" way. Drawing conclusions from the language employed in interviews conducted in wave three, Smith and Snell determine that most emerging adults are indifferent toward religion, perceiving its purpose primarily as a school of morals appropriate to teaching children but unnecessary for a vibrant adult life.[29] One of the interviewees, John, although himself a frequent user of cocaine and marijuana, a rare attender of Mass, and at least desiring to be seen as sexually promiscuous (*claiming* to have slept with over thirty women) has no problem articulating his hopes for his religious self in thirty years: "Dragging my kids to church, sending them to CCD."[30]

More so, the particularities of religious belief seem to matter little to either adolescents or emerging adults. Again, in the most recent wave of data and interviews, emerging adults confess that the vital aspect of any religion is belief in God and general morality.[31] Surprisingly, this indifference to the content of religious belief does not mean that either adolescents or emerging adults are syncretists, combining various religious traditions and practices into their own personal faith or "Sheilaism."[32] Nor for that matter are they "spiritual seekers"[33] or "believers without belonging."[34] Only 5 to 7 percent of adolescents include practices from other religious traditions in their own spirituality, with a slight increase among emerging adults, demonstrative of a decrease in importance of the dominant religion as the young adult differentiates from parents.[35] Even when emerging adults use religious language drawn from other traditions, such as the frequent evocation of *karma* in discussing the need for morality, they do so without serious study or practice of that tradition.[36]

Additionally, adolescents and emerging adults often consent to the religious beliefs and practices of the tradition (however diminished they may be) but do not allow these beliefs or practices to influence daily life. In fact, such beliefs and practices are often limited to the personal and subjective, since the cultural world of adolescents and emerging adults is defined by a kind of relativity, one in which "claims are not staked, rational arguments are not developed, differences are not engaged, nature (as in the natural world, the reality beyond what humans make up) is not referenced, and universals are not recognized." [37] Smith and Snell write:

> Most emerging adults have religious beliefs. They believe in God. They probably believe in an afterlife. They may even believe in Jesus. But those religious ideas are for the most part abstract agreements that have been mentally checked off and filed away. They are not what emerging adults organize their lives around. They do not particularly drive the majority's priorities, commitments, values, or goals. They have much more to do with jobs, friends, fun, and financial security. Yes, basic religious beliefs indirectly help people to be good. But that comes out of deeply socialized instincts and feelings, not anything you have to really consciously think about or actively commit to. In this way, most emerging adults maintain various religious beliefs that actually do not seem to matter much. [38]

Emerging adults are at root religiously indifferent (it's there, we like it well enough, and that's okay), prone to follow personal feelings about religious teaching, and hesitant to perceive religion as a social or institutional phenomenon. [39] Based upon this assessment of the religious or spiritual capital of both adolescents and emerging adults, one comes to an important conclusion regarding American secularization. American secularization is not a marginalization of religion in general from human life. It is, as Christian Smith has concluded elsewhere, a kind of internal secularization whereby the particularities of religious faith, its doctrines and practices, are subordinated in a way both like and unlike American civil religion (religiously universal but politically apathetic). [40] This process of secularization results in a parasitic religious perspective that he calls Moralistic Therapeutic Deism (MTD).

What does Smith mean by this term? First, MTD confesses an existence of a God that has created the world and watches over human existence. This God desires human beings to be good to one another, the foundation of all morality. Further, the ultimate meaning of life is happiness and personal well-being. God only becomes involved in this life when there is problem to be solved. And, those who are good eventually end up in heaven. [41] While the substance of this "creed" (as learned from parents) was first laid out among

Smith and Denton's research into adolescent religious life, the third wave of data has confirmed that this common religious outlook remains prevalent among emerging adults, although under a process of constant refinement through developing adult experience and the growing capacity to articulate religious faith or lack thereof.[42] The purpose of this faith is the fostering of

> subjective well-being in its believers and to lubricate interpersonal relationships in the local public sphere. Moralistic Therapeutic Deism exists, with God's aid, to help people succeed in life, to make them feel good, and to help them get along with others—who otherwise are different—in school, at work, on the team, and in other routine areas of life.[43]

In some sense, MTD is evidence of the success of the liberal Protestant project in the United States in which religious leaders in the early twentieth century succumbed to certain features of modern thought, including individualism or freedom, pluralism and tolerance, democracy, and at least among intellectuals, the elevation of scientific inquiry to religious status.[44] Thus, the religious ethos that Americans inhabit, based upon the discourse of the emerging adults interviewed by Smith and Snell, is defined by "individual autonomy, unbounded tolerance, freedom from authorities, the affirmation of pluralism, the centrality of human self-consciousness, the practical value of moral religion, epistemological skepticism, and an instinctive aversion to anything 'dogmatic' or committed to particulars."[45] But, unlike liberal Protestantism, religious language is no longer characterized by hope in historical progress and commitment to the political aspects of the kingdom of God.[46] Instead, perhaps due to the influence and success of American evangelicalism, religious language and understanding has developed "into a popular mentality about religion that presumes that the sum total purpose and value of religion per se are simply the practical benefits it affords believers. Religious faith becomes good *if* and *because* it makes people do better, if it helps them live more moral lives."[47]

Liturgy and Internal Secularization

Thus, the present obstacle, at least to those seeking to foster the evangelical features of liturgical prayer, is threefold. First, American secularization is an attenuation of the theological imagination. The particularity of the signs of any religious faith ultimately does not matter; for the purpose of all religion is simply belief in the existence of God and a moral life.[48] The narratives and practices of religion are marginal to this broader perspective.

Therefore, to introduce Christians into an approach to liturgical worship whereby one becomes more fully the image of God through meditating upon and appropriating the signs of worship into a way of life is foreign to the modern imagination. We seek worship that entertains, that corresponds to our understanding of God, however limited such an understanding might be. The first goal of any liturgical formation will be to foster a certain facility in the images and practices of Christian tradition, including liturgical rites, the spiritual life, and the narratives and doctrines essential to the sacramental life of the church.

Consider an example prominent in the present Roman liturgy. In the English third edition of the Roman Missal, Eucharistic Prayer II offers the following image: "You are indeed Holy, O Lord, / the fount of all holiness. / Make holy, therefore, these gifts, we pray, / by sending down your Spirit upon them like the *dewfall*" (my emphasis). Such an image has often been perceived as bizarre by those who participate in the eucharistic liturgy of the church. In fact, the most common discussion that I have heard among liturgists regarding the phrase is a scientific quibble about the quaintness of saying that dew "falls" rather than condenses. Such a discussion fails to see that "dewfall" is a scriptural image, drawing the imagination of the Christian into salvation history. In the book of Exodus, when the neophyte nation of Israel wanders through the desert, mumbling in their discontent, God bestows to them manna from heaven. The Latin text of the Bible, the Vulgate, speaks about the descent of this manna from heaven as a kind of dewfall upon the ground—the tradition that Eucharistic Prayer II takes up. Thus, when the church begins to pray that the Spirit will descend upon the gifts of bread and wine, we recall the image of God bestowing the bread of consolation, not because of the worth of Israel (who was already beginning to complain, seeking to return to Egypt where there was meat to consume). Rather, God bestows the gift of this bread out of generosity, a foolish desire to enter into relationship with this people, out of love! Likewise, the Spirit will descend in our eucharistic liturgy *this day,* not because of the worth of the priest, the exceptional virtues of holiness in this assembly, but because the Word has decided to become flesh and dwell among us. Because God is love.

Of course, the richness of a theological imagination is not simply necessary to understand the words of a eucharistic prayer. When I ask my students why they attend the eucharistic liturgy on campus within their dorms, they describe the emotional effect the Eucharist has on their lives; the great preaching they encounter, which is funny and interesting; the dorm traditions of slamming a book shut, singing a hymn as loudly as one can; the strong sense of community that they feel when celebrating the Eucharist in the context of their dorms. These very same students often admit to me that they no longer go to Mass at their home parish because their affections, their desires, the same sense of community are not present. While not dismissing the need for a robust renewal of parish life, the students' decisions are based on a rather thin notion of what liturgical prayer includes. The foreground of their imagination lacks any sense that the Eucharist is first and foremost a participation in the divine life of God, whereby our affections, our desires, even our boredom become an offering to the living God. And when we might feel as young adults that we are a marginal part of the population, we attend the local parish's Eucharist because in this particular community, in the gathering together of the old and the young, the rich and the poor, we slowly learn the art of self-giving love, which we dare to call salvation.

Second, since these signs matter little in the first place, one should not be surprised to perceive a carelessness of theological thinking operative within most religious discourse. The modern religious imagination does not seek a deeper understanding of the signs of belief, of practice—what the church has traditionally called mystagogy. Part of this hesitancy toward seeking understanding in religious belief is an instrumental approach to education in the first place. That is, in college, for example, "what matters is getting the credits, earning the diploma, and becoming certified as a college-educated person so that one can get a better job, earn more money, and become a good salary earner and supporter of a (materially) comfortable and secure life."[49] Questions of meaning are peripheral in such an education. Further, since the particularities of each religion is considered a matter of social construction, disconnected from any claims regarding the way the world really is, then what is the point of asking questions in the first place?[50] Discussion regarding religion seems to generate so little conflict among emerging adults, for example, precisely because the particularities of religious belief are unrelated to a true vision of the world, of oneself, or God.[51] Likewise, an underlying assumption of MTD is a privileging of scientific knowing over the "understanding" one receives through faith. Smith and Snell write, "Science, experiments, research, and people's own personal observations provide solid evidence, most emerging adults think, that certain things in reality are proven, are positive and reliable. Everyone should believe those things. But religion is not like that. It requires what some emerging adults call 'blind faith.'"[52] This privileging of scientific knowledge does not result in a diminution of religious belief for most, precisely because such belief functions to build up subjective well-being, not to make claims regarding reality. Hence, an operative set of doctrines and dogma *does* guide religious belief today, primarily influenced by "individual experience," that which is tangible and visible, over any particular set of traditions.[53]

Of course, this becomes a problem for those seeking to inculcate a mystagogical imagination in a community, one that relies upon a way of knowing that perceives more in the world of signs than what is visible to the eye. To become capable of perceiving a world sacramentally (and thus truly), the Christian will need to permit one's internal narrative or experience to be reformed by the sights of faith. This is a process, which involves reading, understanding, self-examination, and seeking the reality of God through tradition-specific visible signs, and in the process, becoming capable of using the signs to enjoy the reality of God.

Again, let us turn to an example of such a mystagogical imagination drawn from the rites of the church. Much of the church celebrates the feast of the Ascension as a kind of embarrassing, stuttering attempt to explain where the resurrected Christ is now.[54] He is in heaven, dwelling upon some primordial cloud. Yet, the claim that Christ has ascended into heaven, celebrated in every liturgical rite of the church, should produce within us an inquisitive wonder. The opening collect for the feast of the Ascension (At the Mass During the Day) declares, "Gladden us with holy joys, almighty God, / and make us rejoice with devout thanksgiving, / for the Ascension of Christ your Son / is our exaltation, / and, where the Head has gone before in glory, / the Body is called to follow in hope." Jesus Christ is fully human and fully divine. Though he descended as the Word, he ascended into heaven as the Word made flesh, now bathed in resurrection light. Our very flesh sits at the right hand of the Father, his wounds of love still marking his body. Everything that was human in Christ is now in the presence of the Father, without the slightest loss of humanity. The Ascension is the marvelous exchange of human nature and divine life, no longer simply within time but in the eternity to which each of us is destined. All our prayers, our sorrows, and the glory of human life is whispered in the ear of the Father through the mediation of the Son. Every single sign in the liturgical prayer of the church, each human affection, every desire, and the narrative of our lives are in the process of being transfigured through the liturgical prayer of the church.

Finally, American secularization leads ultimately to an exclusive emphasis upon individual flourishing detrimental to the liturgical pedagogy of faith integral to evangelization. Indeed, I need to be careful here in this claim, since I do not want to argue that fruitful liturgical prayer requires self-abnegation to the point of violence or passivity in the face of injustice. Still, the way that religion functions in the lives of both adolescents and emerging adults operates out of an understanding of flourishing, which is too narrow. As Smith and Denton write:

> What legitimates the religion of most youth today is not that it is the life-transformative, transcendent truth, but that it instrumentally provides mental, psychological, emotional, and social benefits that teens find useful and valuable. This is not an unambiguously bad (or good) fact. Most people would hope and expect that religious faith would indeed help youth to behave well, avoid trouble, solve problems, feel supported, and be happy. No American religious tradition actively promotes poor behavior, negative attitudes, and unhappiness. But all major American religious traditions have historically been about more than helping individuals make advantageous choices and maintain good feelings.[55]

The religious lives of emerging adults show a similar correlation between religious practice and individual flourishing. Among those interviewed, few see any problem with consumerism, or demonstrate a commitment to serving one's neighbor.[56] The religious beliefs that they hold function as cognitive placeholders, failing to culminate in transformation of one's fundamental identity. Indeed, this is highly problematic for liturgical prayer. For one's body to become a sacrifice, an offering to God, will require some renunciation of individual flourishing on the part of the Christian. To become the image of God necessitates that the Christian "die" to understandings of what it means to become human (as consumer/producer, for example) apart from the gift of Christ's sacrifice on the cross. Only then will the Christian perceive opportunities for participating in Christ's sacrifice in acts of eucharistic love elicited by all created signs. Only then will liturgical prayer become evangelizing of all culture.

Therefore, a diagnosis of American secularization is fundamentally a matter of an impoverished religious imagination, an interruption of mystagogical desire, and an exclusive focus upon individual flourishing. Indeed, this is the cultural sphere in which liturgical prayer seeks to evangelize, to allow the Word to become flesh in the lives of men and women, schooled in the art of self-giving love. This examination of American secularization may lead us to tremble before the task ahead of us, to wonder if liturgical prayer can do anything at all, when the work is so great. Equally so, there is a temptation, one implicitly present in many liturgical theologians, to assume that liturgy might fix all the problems of the church. That secularity, consumption, injustice, the horrors of war can be permanently healed by eucharistic rites, new hymnody, liturgical catechesis, changing the direction of the altar, and more.

Nonetheless, to dismiss the fallacy of a theology that ascribes too much to liturgical prayer does not mean that the rites of the church cannot contribute to the church's mission of new evangelization. It simply means that the liturgist, the catechist, the priest and bishop, must seek concrete strategies for allowing the liturgical life of the church to evangelize in all of its fullness. We must remove obstacles, reform our own imaginations so that the prayer of the church might reawaken within us the desire for liturgical self-gift; an experience of divine grace, which effects all of our relationships, the way that we perform our job, the manner in which we gaze with love into the eyes of the poor. Such strategic, liturgical formation is requisite for the new evangelization. It is to the development of these strategies to which I now turn.

The Liturgical Homily 3

When teaching courses to undergraduate students on liturgical topics, I have learned not to presume too much regarding their knowledge of salvation history. While some of the major figures in biblical history are known by name, and while students have a general sense of a morality related to the biblical text, they are unable to articulate the underlying narrative of the Scriptures. The creation accounts in the book of Genesis function as an unsophisticated history of the origins of the world. The pre-Exodus foundations of Israel offer quaint morality plays embodied in the lives of Abraham, Isaac, Jacob, and Joseph. The stunning drama of the text, the question of grasping God's exasperating freedom to choose even those who are unworthy goes unnoticed. The liberating history of Exodus and the subsequent foundation of Israel are passed over with only moderate awareness of God's gift of love. The establishment of the monarchy, the arising of the prophetic tradition, the Babylonian captivity, the songs of the Suffering Servant, the disenchantment over an underwhelming second temple, and the expectation of that Messiah who would reestablish the glory of Israel: these vital facets of salvation remain unknown. Likewise, my students employ a series of clichés regarding who precisely Jesus Christ was, ranging from the upright human being to the one who saves us from our sins (not understanding what the latter means). Absent the larger narrative of salvation, they cannot grasp the claim that the liturgical rites of the church are a participation in salvation history. What is this history? And why would we want to participate in it in the first place?

In this chapter, I argue that a deeper attention to the kerygmatic quality to liturgical prayer is necessary for the work of the new evangelization. First, I establish that liturgical prayer, if contemplated with the proper dispositions, enables one to grasp in wonder the central moments of this kerygma in the context of the church's memory. This first argument is made in light of the writings of the liturgical and catechetical theologian, Josef Jungmann,

S.J. Second, I set forth the contours of what constitutes a "liturgical homily" as an essential aspect of articulating this kerygma in a persuasive manner. Lastly, I offer an example of a liturgical homily for the feast of the Nativity of the Lord, which embodies a mystagogical approach to preaching in light of the new evangelization.

Josef Jungmann, S.J.: Liturgical Prayer as Kerygma

Josef Jungmann (1889–1975) occupies an inimitable role in the history of the liturgical and catechetical movements.[1] His research in liturgical and catechetical history and theory set the foundation for both the postconciliar liturgical reform and a renewed catechetical vision. In *The Good News Yesterday and Today*, Jungmann develops an argument for a catechesis of kerygma.[2] In the early church Christian teachers preached the ideals of the Christian life as manifested in the new relationship established between God and humanity in Jesus Christ.[3] The purpose of catechesis in this period was a proclamation of Christian faith, inviting each person to enter into this new life in Christ through an encounter with the Christian narrative.[4] Whereas previous generations of Christians relied on a comprehensive Christian ecology to facilitate the traditioning of this kerygma, Jungmann argues that contemporary catechesis can no longer presume this environment.[5] The context of catechesis in the modern world necessitates that the catechist proclaim the facts of Christianity as a persuasive communication of the "*vital understanding* of the Christian message, bringing together 'the many' into a consistent, unified whole, that then *there may be joyous interest and enthusiastic response* in living faith."[6]

This proclamation is not simply a matter of laying out the essentials of salvation history as recorded in the Scriptures. Catechesis, the homily, religious art, and the liturgical act are oriented toward the proclamation of the Christian message.[7] In particular, the liturgy is the communication, realization, and participation in this message of salvation.[8] As Jungmann writes elsewhere, "At all times the purpose of the liturgy has been to bring the faithful together, so that they might stand before God as the church, as the people of God. But the liturgy has also intended more than this: it has aimed to lead the faithful to a *conscious Christian faith.*"[9] Participation in the liturgy becomes the privileged subject in the curriculum of the school of Christian faith.

Liturgical prayer performs a kerygmatic function in Jungmann's writings, cultivating the Christian in conscious faith in three primary ways. First, participation in the liturgy leads to a participation in the kerygma. Second, the liturgy communicates the doctrine or teaching of Christianity through the media of liturgical prayer. Third, liturgical participation fosters a vision of the world that culminates in a sacramental approach to human life.

An Experience of Liturgical Kerygma

In 1925, Josef Jungmann published his doctoral work, entitled *Die Stellung Christi im liturgischen Gebet* (*The Place of Christ in Liturgical Prayer*).[10] In this classic of liturgical studies, Jungmann argues that up until the fourth century the liturgical presidential prayer did not directly address Christ but God through (*dia/per*) Christ.[11] Since Christians pray through Christ in the context of the church, their prayers "gain meaning and value only because Christ as high priest stands at her head and joins in them."[12] Liturgical prayer is efficacious because Christ is the mediator of this prayer, allowing the church to stand in relationship with the Father in the name of Jesus through praise, adoration, and intercession.[13] This new relationship echoes the proclamation of salvation in which "now there is atonement and peace, confidence . . . and free access to God."[14] The structure of liturgical prayer in the early church is a recapitulation of the event of salvation. By praying in the name of Jesus, liturgy remembers the good news of the redemption of humanity and invites each participant to become a child of God.[15] As Jungmann writes, "it is in the formal prayer of the Christian community that the structure of our relationship to God is directly expressed."[16]

While the early liturgy proclaimed the heart of this christological kerygma with clarity, later historical developments cast a fog over the proclamatory quality of liturgical practice. As a result of the theological battles with Arianism in the fourth century, liturgical prayer addresses Christ directly and in the process favors his divinity over his humanity and role as mediator.[17] This subtle shift in the structure of liturgical prayer, while a consequence of well-intentioned theological adjustments, has a harmful effect upon the participation of the assembly in liturgical rites. As Christ became the addressee of liturgical prayer, the eucharistic liturgy begins to exhibit an almost neurotic concern with the bodily presence of Christ in the Eucharist rather than focusing upon his resurrected and glorified body as mediated within the life of the church.[18] The result of this turn to Christ's eucharistic presence as God among mortals is an emphasis on Eucharist as a sacrificial activity of the priest alone, inducing awe at Christ's presence among liturgical spectators.[19] The only person capable of offering this sacrifice, once performed as a common act of the whole assembly, is the priest. Letting Jungmann speak for himself:

> Only the priest is permitted to enter the sanctuary to offer the sacrifice. He begins from now on to say the prayers of the Canon in a low voice and the altar becomes farther and farther removed from the people into the rear of the apse. In some measure, the idea of a holy people who are as close to God as the priest is, has become lost. The church begins to be represented chiefly by the clergy. The corporate character of public worship, so meaningful for early Christianity, begins to crumble at its foundations.[20]

With the lack of lay participation and an accent upon a eucharistic theology shaped by an overly clerical notion of sacrifice, a host of liturgical problems occur, including a shift away from the Easter motif in Christian proclamation toward an exclusive emphasis on the passion of Christ; the prohibition of the vernacular in the liturgy; a departure from the historical narrative of salvation within liturgical prayer and preaching; and a tendency to privilege devotion to the saints or the Sacred Heart of Jesus over the liturgical year itself.[21] Before the arrival of the modern era, these liturgical deficiencies were counteracted through a Christian culture that embodied this kerygma.[22] The situation of contemporary Christianity in a secular world requires a return to full liturgical participation in order to foster conscious faith.

Liturgical reform is thus a pivotal aspect of the pastoral care of the church in the modern world.[23] Through the reform of the liturgy, the kerygma is once again proclaimed with clarity so that all Christians might realize their own participation in the sacrifice of Christ.[24] The reforms called for by the Second Vatican Council were intended, not as a historical anti-quarianism as Jungmann is sometimes charged by his critics, but a return to a structure of liturgical prayer that Jungmann believed communicated the kerygma of Christian faith.[25]

Learning Liturgical Kerygma

For Jungmann, participation in the sacrifice of praise to God through Christ within the church is the primary function of the Christian liturgy. Still, liturgical prayer is not simply an announcement of the event of salvation but an aesthetic and persuasive entrée into the reality of Christian faith. In *Handing on the Faith*, Jungmann addresses this pedagogical consequence of liturgical participation:

> In the liturgy (as generally in prayer) we approach the truths and the facts of religion with the proper dispositions. In the liturgy we do not

philosophize about God, but we do adore him. In the liturgy we do not attempt to analyse faith, hope and charity, but we practise [sic] them. In the liturgy we avail ourselves of the Sacraments with holy reverence, and we live as children of the church. Although liturgy is not primarily concerned with educating us . . . it, nevertheless, tends to communicate to us those dispositions which are required by the whole of reality which gravitates around God and in this way forms Christian character so profoundly.[26]

The shortened patristic maxim, *lex orandi, lex credendi*, is not only an instance of the liturgy conveying what the church believes, but of liturgical prayer increasing the possibility of faith in the deeds and words of salvation history in the first place.[27] Jungmann's student, Johannes Hofinger, S.J., commenting upon the content of liturgical prayer, writes "The truths of our faith find an impressive, concrete, and even dramatic expression in the house of God with its liturgical objects and actions."[28] In the liturgy, theological propositions and doctrines return to their roots in sacraments and feasts.

The liturgical year is crucial to the function of liturgy in immersing one into Christian faith as an act of aesthetic persuasion. As Jungmann states, "Of all the areas of Christian formation, the church year is the one in which the main themes of the Christian message are most clearly engraved on the souls of the people and in which they are most easily stirred to new life."[29] At Christmas and Epiphany, the church celebrates the event of the incarnation, enabling the priest to preach upon the divine-human exchange accomplished in the incarnation.[30] At Easter, a similar liturgical-kerygmatic moment is available to the church, since the pastor may focus upon the doctrine of grace and salvation in Jesus Christ, as well as the role of the church in living out this new life of grace.[31] Such preaching transpires in the very celebration of these events. The Christian is open to investigating a truth that he or she has savored in the act of celebrating. Formal catechetical instruction (including preaching) "will aim at clarifying the meaningful relationships of the events of salvation and of the church's institutions with the hope that, as instruction progresses, this objective order may find a subjective reflection in the mind of the student."[32]

Liturgical Kerygma as Sacramental Vision

Liturgical participation also forms the person toward a mode of living in the world informed by a sacramental, and thus priestly, vision of human existence. Jungmann shared this interest in connecting liturgy and life with other figures in the liturgical movement, including Lambert Beauduin and Romano Guardini in the European context, and Virgil Michel in the American.[33] As Jungmann writes:

> If the church comes to life in the participants in the actively celebrated liturgy, then a new relationship to the surrounding world comes into being; a new relationship to the material world itself, to the world of trades and professions. For it is real men of flesh and blood who are caught up in the process of the liturgy. It is their voices, their goings and comings which have become part of the sacred action. It is the bread from the work-a-day world which is carried to the altar. It is the work of the trademan's hands which appears in the sacred furnishings and decorations, in the building which encloses everything. It is the every-day world which is drawn into the sacred action, joined with the sacrifice which Christ presents with His Church assembled here.[34]

Liturgical participation leads the Christian to the point of offering his or her life as a sacrifice of praise to God. When Christians participate in this liturgy, they "will come to see that worship—divine service—must be nothing but the distillation of a way of life in which men serve God, that divine service, in the sense of worship, and the service of God must merge into one another."[35] The art of Christian living, one's vocation in the world, and the apostolic mission of all Christians find their source in this new vision of the Christian life proclaimed and taught through liturgical prayer.[36] By becoming an active participant in the Christian liturgy, all Christians begin to live a sacramental and priestly existence; they become themselves a bodily kerygma within the world.

Participation in the liturgical rites of the church is itself an encounter with the Scriptural imagination of the church, a slow meditation upon how humanity has been transformed through Christ's coming to dwell among us. It is that moment in which the church's act of proclamation, of kerygma, becomes anamnesis, a way of ritual remembering whereby we participate in a history that is constantly present to us through the rites of the church.[37] The very action of this prayer forms the Christian in the art of self-gift, as we are immersed in the sacrifice of love bestowed from the Son to the Father. At the same time, our memories, our desires, our very imaginations are enriched through immersion into the christological aesthetics of the liturgical year. Lastly, liturgical prayer enacts the very transfiguration of creation through our bodies, as we are inspired to become self-gift for the world in the particular histories of our lives. We become what we receive in the liturgical encounter, a people made for the harmony of divine praise, one that might woo all of humanity to give of ourselves in love to the very end.

The Liturgical Homily

Jungmann's account of liturgical prayer is an attractive one, fundamental to the renewal of the liturgical rites accomplished at the Second Vatican Council. The vision promoted by Jungmann, one in which the kerygma of the church is not simply articulated but celebrated in all of its living vitality, might serve as an antidote to the Moralistic Therapeutic Deism analyzed in the previous chapter. Yet, as any frequent liturgical participant knows, parish liturgical celebrations do not often live up to this vision. The homily, a central moment in which this vision is often communicated, made present through the sacramental word, fails to promote this imagination.

In the various parishes in which I have been a part, I regularly overhear comments regarding the disorganized quality of the preaching; the way in which the homily becomes not a proclamation of the Gospel but a public therapy session for the priest; the often authoritarian, despairing, or didactic tone of the homilist; the frequent complaint that the homilies remain disconnected from the lives of those attending the Sunday Eucharist. The recent document of the American bishops, *Preaching the Mystery of Faith: The Sunday Homily* (PMF) summarizes the problem well: "in survey after survey over the past years, the People of God have called for more powerful and inspiring preaching. A steady diet of tepid or poorly prepared homilies is often cited as a cause for discouragement on the part of laity and even leading some to turn away from the Church."[38]

If the liturgical prayer of the church is to foster a renewed sense of participating in the mystery of Christ, one that transforms our histories and for this reason becomes a moment within the new evangelization, we will need to improve liturgical homilies. Homilies should lift up the imagination, forming us in a liturgical and doxological way of perceiving our lives. The homily is not an opportunity for informal discourse within the liturgy. It is a liturgical action. I would like to suggest five strategies that the homilist might use in order to enact the remarkable liturgical vision of Jungmann, to preach a kerygma of salvific remembering for the new evangelization: 1) immerse oneself in the scriptural imagination, 2) contemplate the mystery of Christ in the liturgical year, 3) develop an acute sense of human experience, 4) become an expert in doctrine as doxology, 5) learn to read the signs of culture.

Immersion into the Scriptural Imagination

One need not pursue a doctorate in preaching to notice a fundamental reality: Catholic preaching often engages only peripherally with the Scriptures. In my doctoral studies at Boston College, the Jesuit community prided itself on the three-point homily in which systematic or spiritual instruction on certain themes received prominence of place. Likewise, in much parish preaching, the priest's own narrative becomes the center of the homily. Themes from the Scriptures are chosen insofar as they relate to the opening story, and the sometimes shocking images used in the Scriptures are molded to fit the narrative.

The problem with such approaches is *not* that they are ineffective. Homilists who happen to be spiritual masters can often comb the mundane details of their own lives, awakening us to the powerful presence of the triune God who acts in the quotidian. A three-point homily, or developing one or two insights from each reading during Sunday Eucharist, can be formative of a parish's way of thinking. Such homiletic techniques can be effective for catechesis and theological lectures, particularly when engaging with an assembly already attuned to the narrative of the Scriptures.

The drawback is that such homiletic methods are nonliturgical. They do not invite the listener to participate in that divine history, the pedagogy of God, which is at the heart of the liturgical life of the church. Joseph Ratzinger, commenting on this fact, writes:

> Christian preaching does not just tell stories; rather it proclaims a history [*Geschicte*], namely, the history of God with mankind, the process of *transitus*, of the holy Passover, which began with God's call to Abraham. . . . Stories in Christian preaching are not just ornamentation for a non-narrative doctrine; rather, the core itself is history.[39]

In the act of telling the narrative of salvation, Christian preaching invites the assembly to participate anew in the self-giving love of God through the mediation of human speech. The history of salvation, those acts that took place in some remote time, ruminates in the memory of the church and takes flesh again in the hearing of the local assembly. The homilist must know the biblical narrative well enough that he is able to imaginatively enter into the narrative, at the same time that he can communicate the scriptural narrative as event.

If the homily seeks to attune us to the history of salvation, then the first task of the homilist is to immerse himself into this history as proclaimed in the Scriptures of the church. Such an immersion into the scriptural narrative is by no means an easy one. In some ways, it goes against the primary method of formation, which many seminarians receive relative to the biblical text. Historical-critical exegesis of texts alone does not provide the broader narrative present within the Scriptures, the vision of God acting within history embodied in the Lectionary.[40] Because the Lectionary immerses us into the drama of that Christian narrative of salvation unfolding from the very commencement of time, literary approaches to the Scriptures become a necessity for forming the liturgical homilist.[41]

When critiquing or watching a film or a literary art form, it is essential to pay attention to the images, the introduction of specific narratives, even the way that one scene or chapter plays against another. For the Christian, the Scriptures have more in common with a film, a complicated novel, a brilliant symphony with various themes that are introduced and then taken up again throughout the playing of the piece. Indeed, I recognize that this is a controversial claim, one often anathema in contemporary biblical study. The Old Testament should be read, as some might argue, not in light of later readings performed by Christians in the New Testament but on its own. But as the literary critic Northrop Frye points out:

> What matters is that "the Bible" has traditionally been read as a unity, and has influenced Western imagination as a unity. . . . Those who do succeed in reading the Bible from beginning to end will discover that at least it has a beginning and an end, and some traces of a total structure. It begins where time begins, with the creation of the world; it ends where time ends, with the Apocalypse, and it surveys human history in between, or the aspect of history it is interested in, under the symbolic names of Adam and Israel. There is also a body of concrete images: city, mountain, river, garden, tree, oil, foundation, bread, wine, bride, sheep, and many others, which recur so often that they clearly indicate some kind of unifying principle.[42]

The education of the homilist relative to these biblical themes should become an essential part of his formation. For in the liturgy itself, we read the biblical narrative as a unity. During the Easter Vigil, we pray over the baptismal waters, remembering the primordial waters of creation, the flood itself as a sacramental mystery pointing toward baptism, the passing of Israel through the river dry-shod, the baptism of Christ in the Jordan, and the dominical command to baptize all nations in the name of the Father, the Son, and the Holy Spirit. A liturgical reading of the Scriptures necessitates that we begin to notice the themes and images that are taken up throughout the text.

Such homiletic formation need not be difficult. Take for example, the following passage from the book of Genesis: "And the LORD God formed out of the earth all the wild beasts and all the birds of the sky, and brought them to the man to see what he could call them; and whatever the man called each living creature, that would be its name" (Gen 2:19, *Tanakh*). The theme of bestowing a name should not be quickly passed over in the scriptural narrative. On one level, it is remarkable that God gave to humanity the capacity to name in the first place, the ability to gaze at the created order, and then both recognize the wisdom of God and denominate such wisdom.[43] Further, those of us who have read the biblical text are well aware that God changes the names of those who follow him. Even more remarkable within the biblical text, the bestowal of the divine name becomes a climax in the narrative:

> Moses said to God, "When I come to the Israelites and say to them, 'The God of your father has sent me to you,' and they ask me, 'What is His name?' what shall I say to them?" And God said to Moses, "Ehyeh-Asher-Ehyeh." He continued, "Thus shall you say to the Israelites, 'Ehyeh sent me to you.'" And God said further to Moses, "Thus shall you speak to the Israelites: The LORD, the God of your fathers, the God of Abraham, the God of Isaac, and the God of Jacob, has sent me to you: This shall be My name forever, This My appellation for all eternity." (Exod 3:13-15, *Tanakh*)

The God who created the universe, who called forth Abraham, Isaac, and Jacob, now agrees to be "captive" to human speech, entering into a relationship in which Israel might call God by a name, a name that both conceals and reveals who God is: "The name, a sign of acquaintance, becomes the cipher for the perpetually unknown and unnamed quality of God."[44] God's entering into the name marks a new epoch in Israel, one in which the God of Abraham, of Isaac, of Jacob agrees to be with Israel for eternity. The bestowal of a name, even one as complex as God gives, is an agreement to enter into communion, into history. God gives a name that can be offered in prayer, lament, even in human words that curse and despise God.

Of course, God's entrance into the act of denomination culminates in the gift of the Son, the Word made flesh, Jesus the Messiah. The God who bestowed the name in Exodus takes up a name in the Gospels, handing himself over even to the violence of human speech and action. As Ratzinger writes:

> Christ is the true Moses, the fulfillment of the revelation of God's name; he does more than this, since he himself is the face of God. He himself is the name of God. In him, we can address God as "you," as person, as

heart. His own name, Jesus, brings the mysterious name at the burning bush to its fulfillment; now we can see that God has not said all that he had to say but had interrupted the discourse for a time. This is because the name "Jesus" in its Hebrew form includes the word "Yahweh" and adds a further element to it: God "saves." "I am who I am"—thanks to Jesus, this now means: "I am the one who saves you." His Being is salvation.[45]

The God of Abraham, of Isaac, and of Jacob becomes for us the name of our beloved. He returns us to the Paradise of Adam, teaching us again how to name the created order aright. Jesus, who reveals the name of God as triune, takes up human speech and redeems it in the process. And even now, he takes up our name. A careful reading of the Scriptures will notice that so often certain disciples, major figures, are not given a name: the Samaritan woman, the man-born-blind, the two disciples on the road to Emmaus. The Scriptures invite us to allow Christ to name us in the narrative, to see how we are the Samaritan woman, we are those born blind, and we are the two disciples on pilgrimage, encountering the God who has a name.

This capacity to read themes across the Scriptures, to develop competency in such scriptural exegesis bestows to the homilist the habit of telling the narrative of salvation in such a way that we ourselves become participants. In fact, even the homilist who has not been formed in this unitary approach to reading the Scriptures can still learn it through the Lectionary. For example, Cycle C of the fourth Sunday of Lent features the parable of the lost or Prodigal Son (Luke 15:11-31). This parable, because of its popularity, receives a privileged treatment in most sermons. Yet, few connect this gospel text to the Old Testament reading proclaimed at the Sunday Eucharist: Joshua 5:9a, 10-12. This text reads:

> The Lord said to Joshua, "Today I have rolled away from you the disgrace of Egypt." While the Israelites were camped in Gilgal they kept the passover in the evening on the fourteenth day of the month in the plains of Jericho. On the day after the passover, on that very day, they ate the produce of the land, unleavened cakes and parched grain. The manna ceased on the day they ate the produce of the land, and the Israelites no longer had manna; they ate the crops of the land of Canaan that year.

This text addresses Israel's entrance into the Promised Land, their celebration of the Passover, and their last consumption of manna in the desert.

What possible connection does this text have to the parable of the Lost Son? To answer this question requires one to know that the Prodigal Son is often treated according to the motif of a journey—all of us have left God but are slowly brought back through the Father's love to the Promised Land. Simultaneously, one must understand the complaining and mumbling of Israel against God in the desert, their desire to be back in Egypt where at least they had fleshpots to eat from; and God's tender offer of manna from heaven as gift beyond gift, grace beyond grace. This text provides a hermeneutic for interpreting the Prodigal Son as part of the broader salvation history of Israel, a way of understanding the older son's fall from generosity, and an approach of moving beyond a moralistic interpretation that we should be better people. Reading the two narratives together brings to our attention that God does not operate out of a stingy economy but offers the gift of a festal banquet even to those who do not deserve it. We cannot manipulate God, either through the guilt-inducing speech of the older son or the younger son's desire to convince his Father to become a servant. We must give ourselves over to the prodigal logic of a God who bestows manna from heaven, who gives us citizenship in the Promised Land despite our bitter complaining, and who awaits our return even in the present moment. As the psalm acclaims on this day, how can we not "taste and see the goodness of the LORD" (Ps 34:8). This way of preaching moves us beyond telling a simple story, presenting a moralistic narrative, and invites us to participate in salvation history itself. The one who enters into the scriptural imagination of gratitude, of gift proclaimed by the homilist, is well disposed to attend the eucharistic banquet that follows the preaching act.

Contemplating the Mystery of Christ in the Liturgical Year

Josef Jungmann pointed to the liturgical year as the privileged source for learning that divine pedagogy of grace made manifest through the God-Man, Jesus Christ. *Verbum Domini* (VD), taking up this claim, states:

> one sees the sage pedagogy of the Church, which proclaims and listens to Sacred Scripture following the rhythm of the liturgical year. This expansion of God's word in time takes place above all in the Eucharistic celebration and in the Liturgy of the Hours. At the center of everything, the paschal mystery shines forth, and around it radiates all the mysteries of Christ and the history of salvation which becomes sacramentally present. (VD 52)

In the United States, the hinge moments of the liturgical year receive adequate attention in preaching. We know the importance of Christmas and Easter, if only because on these days our churches are often filled to capacity. But *Verbum Domini* is encouraging something more than good preaching on feast days. The liturgical year is to become a scriptural hermeneutic, a way of reading the texts of the Lectionary as centered on the mystery of Jesus Christ, active still in the church's sacramental life.

The preacher must become adept at contemplating the mystery of Christ in the feasts of the church year. The liturgical year does not simply recognize that in a distant past something happened to Jesus Christ, to Mary, or to the rest of the saints. Rather, as Columba Marmion has written:

> Love underlies all Christ's mysteries. The humility of the manger, the
> obscurity of the hidden life, the fatigues of the public life, the torments
> of the Passion, the glory of the Resurrection, all is due to love. . . .
> It is love, above all, that is revealed and shines out in the mysteries of
> Jesus. And it is above all by love that we understand them.[46]

Every deed of Christ's is a mystery, a sacrament of the living God, which simultaneously bestows to us an example of what constitutes a flourishing human life. The wonder of the liturgical feasts of the church is that we are slowly presented with the entirety of Christ's life as a deeper entrée into the mystery of God and human existence. The divine-human exchange, which takes place in every liturgical rite, unfolds in a specific way in the liturgical year.

And thus, the prayer texts of both the liturgical year as well as the various sacramental rites should focus our attention on how we go about reading the Scriptures of the day in preparation for the homily. On the feast of Christ the King in the Eucharistic Preface, we pray:

> For you anointed your Only Begotten Son,
> our Lord Jesus Christ, with the oil of gladness
> as eternal Priest and King of all creation,
> so that, by offering himself on the altar of the Cross
> as a spotless sacrifice to bring us peace,
> he might accomplish the mysteries of human redemption
> and, making all created things subject to his rule,
> he might present to the immensity of your majesty
> an eternal and universal kingdom,
> a kingdom of truth and life,
> a kingdom of holiness and grace,
> a kingdom of justice, love and peace.

Depending upon the year, the Gospel texts to be read at Mass include the judgment of the nations in Matthew 25:31-46 (Year A), the encounter of Christ with Pontius Pilate in John 18:33b-37 (Year B), and the confession of the good thief in Luke 23:35-43 (Year C). In each case, the power of the world is rendered mute before the divine kingship of God, one that becomes manifest in the hungry and the thirsty, in the image of the crucified God who reigns from the throne of the cross. Christ reveals to us what the kingdom is, offering an image of the poverty of human power vis-à-vis the self-gift of the Son. Our priestly, prophetic, and royal identity through baptism is not one that gives us an elevated status before the world. We are to become like Christ the King, seeking to enact a kingdom of truth and life, holiness and grace, justice, love, and peace. And we must learn to recognize the darker side of our own royal status; when we love unto the end like Christ, we may find that there is a cross that awaits us.

The prayers of the liturgical year offer a tapestry of salutary images for the homilist to contemplate in his interpretation of the Scriptures. During the season of Advent, we learn to await the glorious coming of that Christ, who seeks to make us worthy to receive him. At Christmas, we contemplate the image of the Word made flesh, coming to know the depths of love shown by the God who entered into infancy as one of us, already prefiguring his passion, death, and resurrection. In Lent, we begin to perceive how ascetic practice including fasting, almsgiving, and prayer, cultivates a heart worthy to participate in Christ's own mystery of self-giving love most fully revealed in the Easter season. In the Easter season, we turn our attention to that pattern of risen life, to that resurrected posture, which should come to define the life of the Christian. In remembering the saints, we are shown how the ordinary virtues of holiness come to manifest Christ's own life here and now. The homilist, who turns his attention to these texts, is not moving outside the scriptural narrative. He is learning to read the Scriptures aright, to perceive how the mystery of Christ is even now unfolding in the life of the church.

This liturgical reading of the Scriptures, one that invites a deeper contemplation of Christ, may be further developed through reading the great homilies of the patristic, medieval, and modern era. Many homiletic programs involve only cursory attention to the history of preaching. But, for the one preparing the Christmas homily, Augustine's taking up of the images of the Scriptures into a poetic, wonder-filled account of the incarnation, becomes an icon for the homilist seeking to preach on the nativity of the Lord. Quoting Augustine:

The maker of humanity was made human: so that the one ruling the stars might nurse upon the breast; that bread might become hungry, that the fountain might become thirsty, that light might sleep, the Way might be fatigued by the journey; that truth might be accused by false witnesses, the judge of the living and of the dead might be judged by mortal judges, justice condemned by the unjust judges, discipline might be scourged by whips, the grape be crowned with thorns, the foundation suspended upon a limb; that power might be infirmed, health be wounded, that life might die.[47]

Here one encounters a liturgical narrative of the Scriptures in which the Son took up all that it means to be human, and we are invited in wonder to participate in this reality. Already, the passion of Christ, his death and resurrection, are made present in the Son's descent into infancy. Homiletic formation should practice preaching in this manner as a way of taking advantage of the fullness of the liturgical year.

Developing an Acute Sense of Human Experience

Thus far, little has been said regarding the function of experience in preaching. Human experience remains integral to the task of the homilist, who does not seek to parrot the biblical narrative but instead desires to cultivate this assembly, gathered in this time and place, to become a fertile field for the Word to become flesh. Of course, there are false notions of experience employed by homilists. The function of the homily is not to provide a personal narrative in which I, the liturgical participation, am invited to feel *pathos* for you, the preacher. I have often been in parishes in which I feel that I have become the prelate's therapist, giving him an opportunity to discover God's presence acting in his past, attending to the various spiritual malaises that he suffers from.

Yet, the abuse of experience in preaching does not mean that preaching should ignore human experience, treating it as cursory to the homiletic act. *Preaching the Mystery of Faith* states:

> Homilies are inspirational when they touch the deepest levels of the human heart and address the real questions of human experience. Pope Benedict XVI, in his encyclical *Spe Salvi*, spoke of people having "little hopes" and the "great hope." "Little hopes" are those ordinary experiences of joy and satisfaction we often experience: the love of family and friends, the anticipation of a vacation or a family celebration, the

> satisfaction of work well done, the blessing of good health, and so on.
> But underneath these smaller hopes must pulsate a deeper "great hope"
> that ultimately gives meaning to all of our experience; the hope for life
> beyond death, the thirst for ultimate truth, goodness, beauty, and peace,
> the hope for communion with God himself. (PMF 15)

If Christian preaching is to be effective, transformative of the human condition, then it must deal with those universal themes that are at the heart of being human.[48] Such a claim may seem trite. But too often the great hopes of human life, the deepest sorrows of our condition, remain unaddressed in homilies. Marriages commence and end without a word from the homilist about the delights and perils of human love. Adolescents suffer from eating disorders, false images of what constitutes beauty in the first place, without the homilist exhorting us to perceive a form of beauty manifested on the cross. Young couples with children struggle with the pressures and loneliness that too often come with living in suburbia, with expectations to achieve success and wealth, without the homilist providing a more firm hope to believe in. Within each of our communities are the poor, those who have no support system, no way to provide for their children. The presence of the poor, the suffering, the sorrowing are often neglected in homilies, which frequently become panegyrics dedicated to upper middle class family life. The hopes and desires of the world are present in each assembly, yet rarely does the homilist address these in a substantial way. The consequence of such preaching is that our lives, the fullness of what constitutes our humanity, have nothing to do with the eucharistic rites of the church. They are left at the door of our parish, as we escape either into entertaining vignettes of the local prelate's recent vacation or moralistic exhortations to become better people according to the minimalistic vision of Catholic faith offered by the homilist.

Thus, the homilist's developing capacity to attend to the fullness of the human experience, as manifested in the local assembly, is more than an effective rhetorical strategy. Such attention to human experience must necessarily occur in liturgical preaching in which the Christian is invited to offer the entirety of one's life to the Father as a gift of love. Consequently, the liturgical homilist should become an expert in the human condition, aware of the subtle desires that are fertile ground for the enfleshment of the Word in our lives. The liturgical homilist will read literature, watch film, engage with art, read political theory, and listen to his own assembly's interpretation of the Scriptures, as a way of understanding more deeply the depth experiences intrinsic to our humanity.

Doxological Doctrine

In a class that I teach to undergraduates, entitled *Christian Experience: Vocation and the Theological Imagination,* students are a bit stunned when they discover the centrality of Christian doctrine to the course. Many of them have been formed in such a way as to dismiss doctrine as extraneous to a true experience of the Christian life. How can something as esoteric as doctrine be relevant to Christian life, to the art of vocational discernment?

The reticence toward doctrine is evident in preaching itself. Homilies rarely touch upon the particularity of the church's doctrine, afraid to bore listeners, who seek to experience God's grace in liturgical action not a catechism lesson. Such silence is not simply operative on complex doctrinal feasts as the Holy Trinity in which many preachers exhort us to love the mystery of the triune God, even if it is a mathematical puzzle and thus incomprehensible to our imaginations. The dearth of doctrine extends to the most imaginatively rich of the church's teachings, the Incarnation and the Resurrection.

The U.S. bishops' recent document on preaching seeks to respond to this doctrinal desert through emphasizing the importance of doctrine in the preaching act. The document states:

> The doctrines of the church should direct the homilist and ensure that he arrives at and preaches about what is in fact the deepest meaning of the Scripture and sacrament for Christian life. For doctrines simply formulate with accuracy what the Church, prompted by the gift of the Spirit, has come to know through the Scriptures proclaimed in the believing assembly and through the sacraments that are celebrated on the foundation of these Scriptures. (PMF 25)

Notice that doctrine functions in such a way to allow the preacher to discover the deepest meaning of the Scriptures, the participation of humanity in God's very life. Doctrine is doxological, seeking to move the listener to adore God through contemplating the church's teaching. For example, the doctrine of creation is a sign meant to be used to enjoy the mystery of God. Contemplating the signs of the doctrine, one may perceive the sheer gratuity of a God, who creates out of nothing, who shares this creation with human beings through vulnerable love. Because the doctrine of creation is a sign in relationship with other signs, it cannot be read alone. To those Christians whose memory is formed in the incarnation, the divine condescension of creation is recapitulated in the doctrine of the incarnation, *the Word became flesh and dwelt among us* (cf. John 1:14). Such doctrines open our imaginations to a vision of both the Scriptures and the world.

Seeking understanding through contemplating the signs of doctrine is necessary for begetting a truer understanding of oneself and God, an interior illumination that produces exterior deeds of love. To understand the Christian belief that Jesus Christ is fully God and fully human is an exercise in seeking insight into what it means to be God and human. If one thinks of Jesus as halfway human and halfway God, or human in the body but divine in the soul, then the signifying potential of this doctrine is reduced. When Jesus is born in Bethlehem in a manger, hungers for his mother's milk, is lost in the temple, lunches with outcasts, dies upon the cross, it is the Word made flesh who acts. God hungers as an act of love, dies as an act of love, and in the process transforms what it means for humans to hunger, to die, and to love. The understanding pursued through the signs of this doctrine forms the images that each person has of God and the primary narrative of what constitutes authentic human life. Doctrine guards the mystery of God, while also enabling us to speak a word about such a God.

All contemplation of doctrinal signs, all understanding is to culminate in a sacrifice of love toward God and neighbor. To contemplate Christ's descent into hell on Holy Saturday is of course to become familiar with the signs of this teaching (including the doctrines of heaven and hell). But, the contemplation of this doctrine becomes fruitful insofar as the Christian perceives in the sign a divine invitation to worship God through love. Christ descended into the lowest places, into darkness, loneliness. As fully God and fully human, he revealed the depths to which each Christian is called to love. The doctrine of the descent into hell is an invitation for each member of the Body of the Christ, the church, to enter into the hellish places of history, bringing the good news that death and poverty and suffering are not defining of human existence. Love is. The social doctrine of the church emerges from this very teaching. We seek to enter into solidarity with the poor not because of any great virtue on our part, because we embrace a progressive political platform, but because the Word made flesh descended into a very real hell, a place of total desolation, of absence from God.[49]

Such a doxological approach to doctrine cannot help but transfigure the imagination of the preacher and the assembly alike. Doctrine bestows a vision to the preacher to see the Scriptures as proclaiming a narrative, which invites our participation. The use of doctrine in preaching is not intended to turn the pulpit into the classroom. Its proper use enables the preacher and the assembly alike to gaze at the world as it really is: to see all reality ever more truly in light of God. As Evelyn Underhill writes in her own commentary upon the doctrines of the Creed:

> The Creed sweeps us up . . . to God, the objective Fact, and his mysterious self-giving to us. It sets first Eternity and then History before us, as the things that truly matter in religion; and shows us a humble and adoring delight in God as the first duty of the believing soul. So there can hardly be a better discipline than the deliberate testing of our vague, dilute, self-occupied spirituality by this superb vision of Reality. These great objective truths are not very fashionable among modern Christians; yet how greatly we need them, if we are to escape pettiness, individualism and emotional bias.[50]

Without the substance of doctrine, the firm teaching of the church that forms our vision, then the preacher and assembly alike may manipulate reality according to their own image and likeness. Doctrine is real, and for this reason, it is beautiful and doxological.

Analyzing Culture

The problem of culture is by no means new to those engaged in the art of preaching Christianity.[51] Melito of Sardis (d. 180) sought to persuade a primarily Jewish-Christian audience that the proper way to celebrate the Passover could only be understood through a typological reading of the Scriptures.[52] Augustine of Hippo (354–430) responded to an often lax congregation through a brilliant, poetic exegesis of the Scriptures deeply connected to moral formation.[53] John Henry Newman (1801–90) countered the religion of the day—one that was dismissive of any religious practices judged too extreme, too intellectually and morally demanding, too "churchy"—through a close reading of Christian doctrine, the arguments of a natural theology, and a frequent attention to the formative function of liturgical and spiritual practices learned within the church.[54] Effective preachers across history form the imaginations of Christians who find it difficult both to believe and live the central teachings of Christian faith in specific cultural contexts.

For this reason, I often grimace when I hear preachers rely on an overly simplistic condemnation of culture in assessing the difficulty of forming Christians in faith in the present day. "In today's culture, no one cares about the Eucharist." "All the modern world is concerned with is consumption of alcohol and sex." "Teens can't hear the Gospel because of the culture of social media." At least one problem with such attitudes is that it is nondiagnostic. It does not offer an explanation for why it might be difficult to care about the Eucharist, why emerging adults seek some release from daily life through alcohol and drugs, and what sort of desires are met through an often addictive engagement in social media.

A further difficulty with a simple dismissal of culture is that the preacher risks denying the important theological truth that the church is not called to look with suspicion upon the world but rather to read "the signs of the times" (*Gaudium et Spes* 4) of culture, of society in the realistic light of the Gospel itself. This approach to culture does not mean a tacit approval of "the world"—of pornography and sexual abuse, of a form of consumption that reduces the human person to an economic growth model, of the inertia of a Congress that often seeks self-promotion above the common good. The goal is not to reduce the church to the "culture of the day" in an effort to evangelize. Nor for that matter should the preacher seek a blanket condemnation of culture in general. Instead, the preacher seeks to treat culture as a series of signs to be read through the lens of the Gospel in order to discern what primary motivations or desires underlie the various images and practices that constitute the imagination of a specific culture.

Of course, a question remains unanswered: what do we mean by culture? Quoting the Anglican theologian Graham Ward, culture is "certain semiotic systems that produce shared knowledges and values among groups of people, constituting their beliefs about the nature of reality . . . a symbolic world-view, embedded, reproduced and modified through specific social practices."[55] An example illustrating this definition of culture may be something as basic as what it means to call oneself a Bostonian. A Bostonian exists in a world in which you root for the Red Sox, you treat traffic lights as suggestions, and you learn an elaborate system of honks to denote your displeasure while driving.

This definition of culture is in fact somewhat consistent with what early Christianity understood about culture. The function of Christian preaching was to ascribe certain practices, exercises, intended to move one toward that worldview expressed in the church. Culture as a whole was not condemned. Rather, like an acute psychologist, the preacher sought to discern the underlying desire or worldview, and in fact use it in incarnating the Gospel in the present. Such an approach to preaching was known as psychagogy, which according to one recent commentator:

> refers to those philosophically articulated traditions of therapy—common in Hellenistic literature—pertaining to how a mature person leads the less mature to perceive and internalize wisdom for themselves. These traditions . . . stress that for therapeutic speech to be effec-

tive, it must be based on knowledge and persuade by adapting itself
in specific ways both to the psychic state of the recipient and to the
particular occasion.[56]

Psychagogy was thus concerned with how human beings are both persuaded
to the truth of a specific account of wisdom, as well as how the teacher
encourages the student to appropriate this wisdom into a form of life. It
was an education into a way of thinking, desiring, and acting, in which
through the mediation of speech, the student participates in a "critical assessment of prior convictions that as often as not led to their abandonment.
This purification was then followed by positive, constructive exercises that
fostered skills of accurate perception and evaluation to enable students to
perceive wisdom on their own."[57]

In dealing with culture, the liturgical homilist must learn to perceive
himself as a psychagogue, not simply condemning or condoning but analyzing significant cultural trends for the kind of human desires implicitly
present. The homilist must invite participants within the assembly to think
for themselves, to imagine how assumptions regarding reality might in fact
be obstacles to the enfleshment of the Word of God.

Such work requires deep attention to all facets of culture. For embodied
in various cultural expressions (advertising, popular music, and literature)
are certain assumptions regarding reality, which may in fact obscure our
vision of God. The preacher must become an expert in creating speech that
woos us toward this alternative vision of reality, one that does not deny the
validity of culture as an expression of our humanity but seeks to purify it
through the love of the God who became flesh. Rather than offer a blanket
condemnation of culture, the liturgical homilist will turn the imagination of
the assembly toward a critical reassessment of the signs of culture, showing
the assembly how the desire at the heart of this feature of culture might be
transformed through divine love.

Take, for example, a culture, prominent among many young adults active within the church, of elevating sex within marriage to an overly sacral
state. In such imagery, sex within marriage often takes on eucharistic over-
tones, which the physical act of sex (as most married people could testify)
cannot support. The wedding and the consequent marriage bed become
the eucharistic altar in which the bride and the bridegroom unite with one
another in love. Sex is often described by such young adults as the greatest
gift, the source and summit of married life. To a certain extent, this over
sacralization of sex in marriage is an unwise baptism of certain assumptions

regarding married love operative within society as a whole. According to this logic, marriage seeks to complete the spouses, forming them in a union that transcends all time and space; it is the perfect harmony of two souls. In fact, the vocation of a marriage is a far more quotidian affair. Assisting these young adults in discerning the cultural assumptions regarding their theological discourse around marriage (embodied on websites and books that are popular among such students) is the work of psychagogy. The liturgical homilist, who preaches a sermon during the nuptial rites of such a couple, is becoming a psychagogue—wooing the couple to a sacramental and thus more salutary view of married love in Christ.

Of course, the therapeutic function of the preacher is not a more thorough and sophisticated way of condemning culture. Quoting Ward in another context:

> If Christian apologetics is to "speak" to the culture they are addressing, then without the in-depth reading of the culture they will not be effective; people won't listen because the apologetics is not helping them to understand something about that culture that they have not seen before; the apologetics is not helping them to understand the lives, values, activities that socially embed them in a specific cultural terrain. Apologetics, viewed in this way, assists the Gospel in setting people free—from false desires, assumed needs, bewitching ideas, unreflected habits and substitutions for the real objects of their longing—to worship God and recognize the true orientation of the human heart toward such worship.[58]

The capacity for the preacher to become an astute reader of culture, able to perceive both light and darkness in the cultural artifacts of late modern society is thus not a sectarian strategy. Rather, the liturgical homilist seeks to interpret cultural signs as a way of inviting his congregation into a form of authentic worship; an engagement with the world that becomes a self-offering of love, transformative of human life and society alike.

Consider the occasional cultural interest in predictions regarding the end of the world by various native tribes across the globe. For some, the initial reaction to such doom and gloom prophecy might be a quaint ridiculing of such predictions. But, the sporadic interest in end of the world scenarios, reflected in the blockbuster films that populate theatres over the summer, reveals a deeper awareness of the fragility of time. Each one of us is moving toward a moment in time in which we will no longer exist. In fact, the civilizations that we reside within (despite their appearances) are *always* falling apart. The roads that we drive upon gradually crumble under the weight of millions of cars and the severity of winter. The body politic grows fat with practices of power and prestige, often divorced from love and truth. Relationships slowly come to an end, not because of the desires of either partner but as death takes us away from what we hoped would be eternal love. The end of the world is not an imaginative scenario for the Christian but a permanent reality, which we reside within, as we await Christ's transformation of the entire cosmos through the gift of love. We do not react with anxious fear to such a scenario, holding on to a shadow of security at all costs. Even our fear can become gift, a hopeful expectation that God will purify the created order in love.

A Christmas Homily: Mass During the Day

The strategies offered in this chapter *could* renew the homiletic techniques of those preachers interested in fostering the new evangelization through the medium of the liturgical homily. The new evangelization seeks to persuade us, to reform the vision of the assembly so that they might offer themselves in a love first learned through the memory of the church. In the closing section of this chapter, I want to provide an example of one such homily, employing the five strategies outlined above, for the Feast of the Nativity of the Lord or Christmas at Mass during the day.

* * * *

In the beginning was the Word, and the Word was with God, and the Word was God. He was in the beginning with God. All things came into being through him, and without him not one thing came into being. What has come into being in him was life, and the life was the light of all people. The light shines in the darkness, and the darkness did not overcome it. (John 1:1-5)

For the most part, our celebration of the feast of Christmas often passes over the darkness. The joys of family celebrations, the anticipation of gifts to be opened, the splendid dress of those gathered in church. Insofar as these traditions help us to celebrate the Word's enfleshment among us, not simply in the stable at Bethlehem but in the church here and now, they are very good things. But, they can become idols, distracting us from the truth that Christmas proclaims: *in the small child born in the Bethlehem stable is the light that shines into the darkness.*

This great truth requires that our contemplation of Christ in Christmas acknowledge the darkness. For in each of our parishes, there are those that know only darkness. The young mother with three children who must suffer the abuse of her husband may see only the darkness. The couple unable to have children may perceive in the feast of Christmas a reminder of their own infertility, and thus may see only the darkness. The elderly husband who just lost his wife and seeks to get through the holiday without too much pain, may see only the darkness. The family of undocumented immigrants in the United States may know only the darkness of fear, of poverty, of deep loneliness. The young woman, who hates her body so much that she continues to harm it through cutting and vomiting up everything that she eats, may know only the darkness. The Wall Street banker, who gets up each morning only to increase his own profit and prestige, may at times look at himself and know only the darkness. The poor, who feel desperately out of place amid those dressed in their finest Christmas clothes, may know only the darkness.

I often think about those who dwell at darkness in the midst of this season of Christmas. For Christmas is the feast for them in particular. The light shines into the darkness, *which of course means that there is darkness for the light to shine into*. Christ comes to embody the very good news that God dwells among us. His advent into the world has not resulted in the erasure of darkness but rather an enlightening of it. For that infant, fresh from the womb, would one day be laid into the tomb. He is to be the despised, rejected, the suffering servant of Good Friday.

Christmas is the feast of God's love among us through Christ, his descent into the darkness of the human condition, and his enlightenment of human history. From the moment that the child was born in Bethlehem, darkness met its match. Not because the infant passes over the darkness as if it did not exist. Rather, *that child* will transform the darkness through the light of love, through self-gift. He will himself encounter darkness: the darkness of infancy and speechlessness; the darkness of the flight into Egypt; the darkness of temptation; the darkness of Gethsemane; the darkness of Calvary. And through his church, he will continue to know the depths of darkness. The martyrdom of St. Stephen, the persecution of St. Paul, and all the darkness that we endured in the twentieth century! Jesus Christ reveals to us that the only way to conquer the darkness is through the light of a descending, self-offering love.

So let us not forget those who dwell in darkness during the feast of Christmas. For Christmas is the season of darkness. But, it is the season in which darkness meets its match in a love akin to the first rays of dawn that pierce the horizon after a cold winter night.

Of course, our reception of this divine love at Christmas does not mean that we must be passive to the darkness. The woman in the abusive relationship needs to seek help. The teen suffering from hatred of self ought to find the light. The banker who pursues a selfish, socially harmful way of life needs to recognize the futility of his pursuit. But, in Christmas, we come to see that these actions are always more than human effort alone. Rather, they are the inbreaking of that Light which is the source of all light into the human condition.

For is this not the very meaning of redemption, the Good News that the season of Christmas inaugurates? We are no longer held captive to the darkness. The darkness of death and sinfulness and power and prestige is not defining of our existence. Rather, love alone is. And we come to know this, to perceive the possibility that God might enter into my darkness through the feast of Christmas. No matter how dark it gets; no matter how little I view the value of my own flesh, my history—God seeks to enter into it. Indeed, we can glimpse here how Christmas may in fact be the best of news to those who "sit in darkness and death's shadow" (Luke 2:79). Only our growing capacity to see this light will "guide our feet into the path of peace."

Liturgical homilies remain integral to the work of the new evangelization. Through the gift of human speech offered by the homilist, the assembly is invited to participate in the liturgical memory of the church, to enter into that kerygmatic proclamation that transforms life itself. In order to offer liturgical homilies that might contribute to the new evangelization, the homilist will need to immerse himself into the scriptural narrative, one that becomes incarnate in the church's liturgical year. Likewise, the homilist will become an expert in human experience, perceiving how the doctrine of the church offers an authentic vision of reality. Simultaneously, liturgical preachers will become adept at cultural analysis, that is, psychagogues who seek to inspire Christians for self-giving love in the context of our social lives.

This renewal of liturgical preaching is, of course, not simply reserved for the ordained, liturgical preacher within Catholicism. The catechist, even the lay preacher, will employ such strategies in order to offer salutary images and narratives for the renewal of the church and the world. The gift of such preaching, if it is practiced within our assemblies, will be a deeper awareness of how the Scriptures are more than quaint stories but the very Word of God, seeking to woo us back to the Father in love.

A Eucharistic Vocation 4

What am I going to do with my life? This question is asked often enough to paralyze us with fear. As adolescents transition to college, they begin to wonder what careers they might undertake. Simultaneously, the question of love and total commitment to a person becomes a pressing one as we consider who, when, and if marriage should become our vocation. As we advance in our professions, in our lives as Christians abiding within the world, the question still calls out to us. Is this an authentic way of living? Is there another position, another way that I might contribute to the world? At retirement, as we approach the end of our involvement in the working world, the questions continue. What has my life meant? Have I given myself fully in relationships and career alike? How will I enter into death, the last great stage of my life, as an act of love?

The question of intentionality in life and of vocation is an existential one, occupying seminars and discussions in colleges and universities throughout this country. Such colleges and universities are concerned that many students enter school, giving themselves over to the logic of the economy before they have begun to discern what enables them to flourish as human beings. But for Christians, the question takes on a deeper meaning. Somehow, we make the audacious claim that the materiality of our lives, our very histories, are being created and re-created by the triune God. Yet, we must slowly become aware of the presence of this God acting within the contours of our lives so that we might live our vocation as a eucharistic offering to the world. Indeed, this turn to vocation is a felicitous one relative to the new evangelization. If the new evangelization requires that we attend to the deepest desires of the human heart, allowing them to become "transubstantiated" through the eucharistic memory of the church, then nothing is more important than the very historical context in which we live as creatures made to adore the living God.

In this chapter, we turn to a deeper consideration of the eucharistic, and thus liturgical, vocation of each Christian as an integral aspect of the new evangelization. The question of Christian vocation takes on a distinctive shape when discerned through the liturgical life of the church. In the first part of this chapter, I offer a description of discernment as developed from the Anglican theologian, Mark McIntosh. In the second, I turn to a mystagogical unfolding of the Eucharistic Prayer as a paradigm for a discerning pattern of life.

Discernment as a Pattern of Life

When a friend of mine, previously unaffiliated with Catholic universities, was offered a job to teach in such an institution, he was told that he would be given some time to discern whether to take the position. According to this friend, reared in the practices of business in the United States, he found the language slightly strange. What could discernment mean? Why were those affiliated with a Catholic university so quick to employ the word when a term such as "decide" might have worked just as well?

Grasping a definition of both vocation and discernment seems essential to the project at hand. In Edward Hahnenberg's recent account of vocation in the Christian life, he provides two such definitions. The language of vocation, for Hahnenberg,

> recognizes that our decisions come as a *response* to something or someone beyond. To speak of a call is to acknowledge a caller, to see that God's gracious initiative precedes all of our projects and our plans, that our individual journeys have a goal. Our freedom does not hover over an infinite number of options (the fundamental paradigm of choice). Our freedom stands under and before the transcendent, always being drawn up and out into the source of our being (the basic pattern of call). How will I respond in love to the God who is love? Unlike the commandments of the moral law, which are meant to mark the floor below which love should never fall, vocation has to do with the wide-open space above. Love has no ceiling, and so my vocation is, quite simply, the way that I will rise.[1]

Vocation is directed toward the transcendent, toward a narrative of love that is outside of ourselves but comes to orient each moment of our lives. The language of vocation is not simply reserved for our career or our calling to religious life, to marriage, or to being single. A robust theology of vocation places the human being before the very fact that the God who dared to enter into human history continues to do so at the microscopic level of my day-to-day affairs.

If vocation is the theological term proper to God's acting in human history, then discernment is the way in which we know of God's action in the present. It is a theological epistemology, a way of knowing infused by an awareness of God's presence. Hahnenberg writes, "discernment is a process of reflecting on my fundamental identity before God. Each of us decides what to do by placing particular possibilities for life before this fundamental sense of ourselves, listening for either resonance or dissonance. Harmony between the two helps us know what we are called to do."[2] In my unofficial responsibility as a spiritual advisor to undergraduates (as theology professors tend to become), I often encounter students torn between the desires they have to serve the church through priesthood or through a vocation to the married life. They await some external and physical call, some tangible evidence of God's plan for their lives. What they do not yet realize is that God's call is taking place through the concrete desires, affections, and historical moments of their lives, if only they were attentive to God's working. Further, there is an elemental, fundamental call constantly available through the very narrative of salvation, which the church continues to ruminate upon in the liturgical rites. Discernment is a way of shaping our lives so that they might become a participation in the paschal mystery, in the death and resurrection of Christ that is to define each moment of our lives.

This work of discernment is by no means simplistic or easy. In advising undergraduates, I often encounter "discernment junkies," who are incapacitated to commit to anything that might be long term, preferring the chaos of a life in the unknown. Years of priestly discernment are abandoned once a potential spouse comes along, only for this very same young man to end the relationship once it becomes too difficult. Students commit to one service program, only to move to another once they no longer feel excited about the first. They seek to leave behind their Catholic identity because the simplistic faith inculcated in childhood does not make sense in a life of complexities of adult life; they no longer "feel" faith.

Indeed, the movement of our affections and our desires are part of God's formation of the human heart. But we can lie to ourselves, perceiving reality not as it is but as we would like it to be. Discernment requires a formation of the discerning subject, a way of learning to see the world, including our own interior life and narrative as it is. It necessitates that we begin to gaze upon our lives, not through those images that we find most comforting, most consoling, but through the eyes of the absolute, self-gift revealed in the Son.

Few have treated the christological nature of discernment more thoroughly than Mark McIntosh in his *Discernment and Truth: The Spirituality and Theology of Knowledge*. In the first chapter of this text, McIntosh sets forth a fivefold pattern to the discerning life. His approach is unique in that he does not ground discernment first and foremost in the object to be discerned but instead focuses on the formation necessary to become a competent discerning subject. As he writes:

> teachers of discernment are wholly united in calling for a patient and persistent attention to the discerning *subject*. By this they do not mean to give priority to the knowing human subject, as in modern epistemology, but on the contrary to emphasize that human knowing needs to be pried loose from the habits of mind it has fallen into and to be completely transformed and attuned to the realities of faith.[3]

McIntosh is pointing us to a pivotal insight. The discerner's natural capacity to know and love God is often thwarted by habits of knowing, ways of being in the world, which do not allow us to encounter reality in its fullness. Many of my students, although unaware of it, are formed into specific habits of mind that make the process of discernment difficult. They believe that God is revealed solely through affections of joy and pleasure rather than dryness and boredom. Many are sure that the final end of human beings is nothing less than success in business and family alike. They discern in the context of a God who does not demand much of humanity in the first place. Such habits of mind stultify discerners, preventing them from perceiving God's work in the world.

The formation of a discerning subject must then begin with renewal of the person through an encounter with the sacramental logic of the paschal mystery itself. At the heart of reality is the triune life of God reflected in "a world whose deep structure and meaning reflects that trinitarian life."[4] The created world is a gift bestowed to us, reflecting the generous economy of a God who loves unto the end. Yet, our eyes are not prepared to perceive the fullness of this generosity insofar as our "hearts are gripped with a mentality of deprivation, suspicion, and scarcity."[5] We are a community of those who line up on Black Friday to grab every last deal, even if we must commit violence upon our neighbor in the process. We engage in a politics that views our fellow member of the *polis* solely through the lens of suspicion and condemnation, a vision that erases his or her humanity. We profess faith in an economy of scarcity, of endless consumption that falsely promises to make us whole. Christian life interrupts such false ways of looking at the created order as the Christian subject is knit into the prodigal economy of the triune God through meditation upon Christ's death and resurrection. McIntosh comments, "By condensing the whole mystery of divine self-giving on the cross, Christ restores to human minds a glimmering of the true principles of the whole cosmic order. 'All things appear in their proper colors' now because they can be seen in terms of the flowing divine life-sharing incarnate on the cross."[6] We commence discernment through the lens of a theological, paschal way of relating to reality, precisely because it orients us toward authentic relationship with the created order:

> It is by coming to partake in all things as this infinite, delighted giving that humanity begins to acquire discernment. It is a profoundly communal vision of reality; shared in love, animated with an intense desire to communicate joy and delight. This transformed vision bestows upon believers a discerning eye to see the world in truth as an event of abounding communion, to see it truly therefore because one sees it as being for joy and one receives and gives the divine joy that pulses as the heart of it.[7]

Through contemplating the particularities of Christian faith embodied in the Scriptures and tradition, and through participation in the paschal mystery, we are gradually formed to view the created order through divine eyes. Our imagination regarding what is possible in the world is renewed. We know the will of God not as something external, thrust upon us as a foreign law from a totalitarian dictator but as a joyful gift from the source of reality itself. We respond by offering our wounded hearts to the Father through the Son in the unity of the Holy Spirit. Discernment begins as a eucharistic gift in which we perceive the wonder of the created world flowing from the bountiful goodness of God, and we offer that return gift of love to the God who created and re-creates us. We join Augustine, who after his conversion, said "Childlike, I chattered away to you, my glory, my wealth, my salvation, and my Lord and God."[8]

Even if transformative participation in the paschal mystery is at the heart of discernment, one must still engage in the difficult work of cultivating self-knowledge in light of this mystery. McIntosh's second moment in discernment is that of distinguishing good and evil impulses. He writes, "Discernment can only deepen if it leads believers to greater awareness of the *lesser desires* that sometimes captivate and distort perception—and so render believers' judgment impermeable to the light of the Spirit."[9] Simply, we do not always understand why we desire certain things. Take the example of me, your author. Presently, I sit before a computer on a gorgeous summer day, writing this text. Part of me is composing this work because I hope that the words might be salutary for those who work within the church, seeking to cultivate the new evangelization through the liturgical rites of the church. Yet, another part of me is writing the book out of a desire to be praised for the pleasantness of my prose. I write to become recognized as a scholar, teacher, and one who might influence the church in some tangible way through *my* ideas. Indeed, we as human beings engage in any number of activities for mixed motives. On this side of the eschaton, we are not yet capable of perceiving the world entirely as gift, of offering our lives in the purity of a love that knows no bounds. If the cross provides us with a vision of all reality as participating in the total gift of love at the heart of the cosmos, it simultaneously calls us forth to open our hearts to the fact that we are still being formed in the image and likeness of God. We must, within the community of the church, discern the spirits that operate within us, to look at ourselves honestly and see where we hold on to grudges, to anger, to perversion of sexual desire, to forms of implicit violence that manipulate our friends, our spouses, and the world itself—bending everything to our limited vision of the world. Authentic discernment necessitates a rather hopeful turn of our whole selves toward the paschal love of the Father and the Son and the Holy Spirit, one that enables us to see how pride, injustice, and self-importance continue to plague us in our journey toward the triune God.

Of course, discernment does not simply operate at the level of the interior life and to addressing the shortcomings of a community's commitment to divine charity. Discernment fosters a habit, a prudent way of abiding in reality, which seeks what is good, perfect, and pleasing to the Father of life in every moment. McIntosh calls this third movement discretion and practical wisdom. He writes:

> . . . discernment as discretion is not simply a matter of having sufficient experience of life that one grasps intuitively the most fitting means to good ends. Rather we are considering here a kind of friendship with the divine orderer of all things sufficient not only to recognize the most fitting means in any given situation but also such that one has the desire and actual capacity to pursue that practical wisdom.[10]

Those schooled in the church's liturgy turn to God in prayer in the morning not because we are required to do so but because we have become habituated to offering words of praise and thanksgiving to the living Son in response to the gift of the new day. The encounter with suffering and sorrow that inevitably marks our lives does not lead members of the church into a narcissistic pity but opens us up more deeply to participate in the mystery of Christ's death. The pastoral minister schooled in the art of discernment encountering a young couple whose attendance at Sunday Eucharist is sparse to nonexistent, knows how to respond in a love that seeks to woo our fellow sojourners back to ecclesial life in the midst of wedding preparation. Discernment seeks to cultivate habits of prayer, love of neighbor, and "a deep capacity to recognize and respond to the divine will in everyday existence."[11] The well-formed discerner acts out of an infused habit of love.

The fourth moment that McIntosh highlights, seeking the truth of God's will, is a bit more difficult. McIntosh states:

> This discernment of the true divine intention in all things seeks to make that truth more visible, more luminous, as the beauty of holiness. We might think of it as a contemplative rediscovery of the right use of all creation and an active capacity to bring all things toward the purposes for which they were intended. Patristic writers such as Origen and Evagrius will call this a form of natural contemplation, a discernment of the true meaning, the inner divine intention or *logos* expressed in and as each creature. . . . This form of discernment also requires some personal relationship and communion with the divine speaker of all things, and a desire to bring that authoring and therefore authoritative speaking to ever greater expression in the world.[12]

An example might be of assistance. Many of us recognize a tendency in present-day American life to do everything we can to escape death, to see our dying as a tragic flaw that must be fixed. Magazines prominently placed on shelves in supermarkets present us with images of men and women whose faces and bodies exhibit an impossible agelessness. Physicians view the death of their patients, no matter their age, as a failure of the scientific and technological innovations they bring to their craft. Those who are elderly, whose death is imminent, are placed far away from mainstream society. Yet, to the Christian formed in the art of discernment, death is not a flaw, something to be avoided at all costs. Death is seen as a participation in Christ's own life, greeted as a gift not to be sadistically savored but offered up in love. In a lovely text, Hans Urs von Balthasar writes regarding a Christian's perception of death, "from this mystery of the life of God, one can see that the natural death of creatures, too, can be a parable of God . . . and most certainly that Jesus Christ can imprint upon worldly death something of the trinitarian life of self-abandonment." [13] At the heart of our death, to the one whose eyes have been formed in Christ's own self-gift, we can see an image of divine love. To the one formed in this way, death is changed forever. Indeed, this moment of discernment is difficult, requiring a rather deep experience of the Christian life. It is a discovery of a truth that could not have been discerned apart from participating in the triune life of God. For those of us who know that death is an experience of the triune love of God spilled out into the world, our practice of life itself is changed. Discernment is a difficult education into such divine truths, a formation that fosters insights that allow us to perceive the world more truly, to recognize the light of life where others can see only the darkness of despair. This education refreshes our patterns of speech and action in such a way that we begin to embody the truth we have contemplated in love.

The last moment of discernment for McIntosh is the contemplation of wisdom. He writes:

> I am suggesting here that the fifth moment of discernment is a contemplative wisdom, born in the paschal mystery, touched by the perfect self-sharing of the divine communion, and able to reconceive the world in ways that hold it open to that limitless life for which it was created. Unless discernment is deeply oriented to this contemplative vision it is easily taken captive by the urgency of more apparently useful works of knowledge.[14]

This way of knowing is ultimately oriented to the eschatological, to a vision of creation in which we perceive all reality as moving toward its final end of union with God. To a certain extent, the fullness of this reality will only be discovered in the beatific vision, in which we gaze upon God face-to-face. Literature has often captured this final moment of discernment in a way that even the finest of theological tomes cannot. In Marilynne Robinson's *Gilead*, the protagonist John Ames, an elderly minister approaching death through writing a journal to his young son, declares to the reader:

> It has seemed to me sometimes as though the Lord breathes on this poor gray ember of Creation and it turns to radiance—for a moment or a year or the span of a life. And then it sinks back into itself again, and to look at it no one would know it had anything to do with fire, or light. . . . Wherever you turn your eyes the world can shine like transfiguration. You don't have to bring a thing to it except a little willingness to see. Only, who could have the courage to see it? [15]

Those practiced in the art of discernment and learned in the wisdom of self-gift no longer need to search with frenetic pace for the will of God acting in the world. Every encounter with creation, even those infused with suffering and sorrow, becomes a revelation of that divine love.

What is so stunning about McIntosh's account of discernment is that it locates vocation within the Christian life as a whole. The practice of discernment forms us to perceive reality as it is, as a gift to be received from the triune God, and then offered back in eucharistic love. This is the heart of Christian vocation, of that participation in the paschal mystery of Christ that comes to inform our identity. Such a way of seeing must be learned, and although McIntosh does not attempt it, perhaps the liturgical and sacramental life of the church is integral to this formation. The liturgical and sacramental rites of the church, if they are to become essential to the mission of the new evangelization, will necessarily inculcate us into their own peculiar grammar of discernment. I now turn to a closer attention of how the Eucharistic Prayer forms us in a discerning pattern of life.

The Pattern of Eucharistic Discernment

The Method of Practice

To a certain extent, we have already treated in chapters 1 and 3 a robust vision of liturgical prayer as enabling us to participate in the paschal mystery of the triune God, the soothing kerygma that passes over into a way of remembering that heals our soul. Yet, the liturgical rites of the church are not simply ideas, a backdoor into communicating theologically informed information to a receiver-participation. The liturgical life of the church is a bodily exercise, a concrete engagement of our affections, our desires, our entire selves in the triune life of God. The rites of the church are not simply reducible to the words of the prayers that we offer, the rubrics and instructions that inform the rite, even the various ministers who contribute to the liturgical event itself. At its root, liturgical prayer is performed by specific actors in time and space, whose practice of the liturgy comes to renew their own understanding of what it means to be Christian.

For this reason, the one who writes about liturgy is faced with a rather complex task: how does one present a discourse on something that is primarily meant to be experienced? A theologian must make decisions, some more adequate than others. In this case, I seek to analyze the Eucharistic Prayer as a practice that orients the Christian into a discerning pattern of life, a way of perceiving reality as participating in the self-giving love of the triune God. Yet, before proceeding, it seems wise to say a word about the use of the term "practice."

In popular discourse, when considering the word "practice," we often contrast it to theory. We desire a *practical* approach to liturgical and sacramental formation. We seek concrete best *practices* that will improve the catechetical or liturgical life of a parish. Theory and the analysis of historical structures are considered *at best* helpful and at worst a mind-numbing exercise that makes our work too complex.

Alternative approaches to practice exist. Dorothy Bass and Craig Dykstra have addressed the theological and anthropological qualities to "practice" in a way that is conducive to our analysis of the Eucharistic Prayer below. They write, "By 'Christian practices' we mean *things Christian people do together over time to address fundamental human needs in response to and in the light of God's active presence for the life of the world.*"[16] They unfold this thesis in four parts.

Christian practices "address conditions fundamental to being human—such as embodiment, temporality, relationship, the use of language, and mortality—and they do so through concrete human acts joined inextricably to substantive convictions about how things really are."[17] Marking time through the liturgical year, for example, occurs through a variety of domestic and ecclesial practices, ranging from decorating one's home in the days after Thanksgiving to having a lit Advent wreath placed prominently in one's kitchen. A human need to live within the concreteness of time and space is met, while simultaneously the Christian family expresses that all time is oriented toward the coming of Christ through the bodily practice of lighting the wreath. Such practices are not merely the communication of information. They inscribe a certain way of life, of engaging in religious life, upon the practitioner.

Christian practices also form the Christian in knowledge of God and oneself.[18] At one level, practices provide for the Christian a new way of being, of living in the created order. Bass and Dykstra propose that "entering the Christian practice of healing . . . develops in the practitioners certain skills, habits, virtues, and capacities of mind and spirit."[19] The practice of praying while walking, for example, leads one to deeper attentiveness to the created world, developing the habit of entering into the prayer each time we walk. The mind is turned toward the mysteries of divine love simply through the act of walking. Likewise, Christian practices provide us with intimate, experiential knowledge of God. Dykstra and Bass write:

Christians who keep holy a weekly day of rest and worship acquire through the Christian practice of sabbath-keeping an embodied knowledge that the world does not depend on our own capacity for ceaseless work and that its life is not under our control. Observing sabbath on the Lord's Day, Christian practitioners comes to know in their bones that creation is God's gift, that God does not intend that anyone should work without respite, and that God has conquered death in the resurrection of Christ. And this knowledge is not only embodied; the words of liturgies, the songs of people gathered for worship, and the difficult decisions that must be made about the actual characteristics of a "holy" day are an intrinsic part of this practice.[20]

Such concrete practices write upon our bodies certain ways of living within the world. Liturgical prayer, suffused with such practices, will form us toward a more authentic way of perceiving the created order through divine eyes and thus enabling our vocational discernment.

Bass and Dykstra point toward two other pivotal features of Christian practice that deserve mention. Practices are "patterned activities carried on by whole communities of people, not just in one particular location, but across nations and generations."[21] Christian practices are not individualistic, to be performed in solitude. They are ecclesial, embodied in the history of a church that connects us to those who have lived patterned lives of discipleship before us. They have prescribed such practices, often because they are aware (when we are not) that these practices are salutary for our condition. Indeed, a Christian may pray at any time, in any place, but there is wisdom to offering Lauds at the rising of the sun. Of course, not all Christian practices actually embody such wisdom. Bass and Dykstra write, "any given practice—including any practice that is historically Christian—can become so distorted that its pursuit and outcome are evil rather than good."[22] Christians who participate in liturgical prayer may see their work not as learning the eucharistic logic that is the triune God but instead may seek to placate God through weekly attendance, manipulate an encounter with some image of the sacred that they themselves have constructed. In such cases, practices may need to be reformed and renewed, and our understanding refreshed through further formation.

Bass and Dykstra's treatment of Christian practice reveals a mystagogical schema for treating the rites of the church. Infused within the liturgical practices of the church is wisdom, a way of being human in the world that orients us toward the triune God. These liturgical rites may become vocational, forming us with insights and habits of mind that orient us toward a new way of perceiving and acting in the created order. By analyzing the human needs, virtues, dispositions, and desires that liturgical rites infuse within us, we may come to see how full, conscious, and active participation in these rites form us in a discerning pattern of life.

The Eucharistic Vocation of the Christian: The Eucharistic Prayer

Consider for a moment the various actions that we perform in each eucharistic liturgy. We enter the church dipping our fingers in the baptismal waters, signing ourselves with the cross. In moments of boredom or silent wonder (depending upon our mood), our eyes are elevated to the incarnate light of stained glass windows and incense rising above the altar. We sing hymns of praise and lament to the living God, the entirety of our speech being offered in prayer. We listen to sacramental words uttered in the poverty of human speech.

The Eucharist is full of a variety of practices, human actions offered to the triune God that reveal the wisdom of Christian living, the pattern of a life given over to divine worship. Yet, no practice is more important within the eucharistic liturgy than the Eucharistic Prayer itself. The *General Instruction of the Roman Missal* (GIRM) states:

> Now the center and high point of the entire celebration begins, namely, the Eucharistic Prayer itself, that is, the prayer of thanksgiving and sanctification. The Priest calls upon the people to lift up their hearts toward the Lord in prayer and thanksgiving; he associates the people with himself in the Prayer that he addresses in the name of the entire community to God the Father through Jesus Christ in the Holy Spirit. Furthermore, the meaning of this Prayer is that the whole congregation of the faithful joins with Christ in confessing the great deeds of God and in the offering of Sacrifice. The Eucharistic Prayer requires that everyone listens to it with reverence and silence.[23]

Notice that offering the Eucharistic Prayer is not simply the responsibility of the priest alone. It is not an occasion for the laity to begin to muse over the various tasks of the day to be completed. Instead, the entire people of God are taken up into the practice of this prayer. This great oration is prayed by those gathered in the assembly.

The eight parts of this prayer (thanksgiving, acclamation [or *Sanctus*], epiclesis, institution narrative or consecration, anamnesis, oblation, intercessions, and concluding doxology) reveal to us what a eucharistic life consists of. By attending to these eight parts, we begin to see how offering this prayer in the assembly of the church reveals the fullness of our vocation as Christians to give thanks and sanctify the cosmos.

Before considering these eight parts, let us turn first to the dialogue that begins the Eucharistic Prayer. The dialogue commences by exhorting us to lift up our hearts. When teaching eucharistic theology to undergraduates, I have often encountered a rather literal interpretation of this appeal, a kind of deafness to the metaphor being employed. In fact, a disposition, the liturgical vocation of the Christian, is summed up by this terse exhortation. Augustine, often preaching on this phrase in his sermons, urges:

> Let us love him and imitate him [Jesus Christ]; let us run after his sweetly scented ointments, as the Song of Songs suggests: *We shall run toward the fragrance of your ointments* (Song 1:3). He came, he spread his sweet fragrance, and his scent has filled the whole world. Where did such scent originate? In heaven. Follow him to heaven, then, if you are not lying when you make your response to the invitation, "Lift up your hearts. Lift up your thoughts, lift up your love, and lift up your hope, lest it go bad on earth." [24]

Augustine's reference to heaven is not a denial of the necessity of abiding in the present, a dig against the materiality of creation. Instead, it is a matter of reorienting our desires as creatures made to praise God. What we love is crucial; and if we love the wrong things, then our desires are turned inward, becoming decayed. To lift up one's heart is to reorient our lives toward worship, to the spirit of praise and adoration that is to define the Christian life. The heart is nothing less than the seat of human affection, of desire, our thoughts and our conscience. The Christian is invited to meditate upon our lives through the exhortation: have I lifted up my desires, my affections, even the entirety of my being to God? When we proclaim that we have lifted up our hearts to the Lord, we are obligating ourselves to a way of life embodied in this Eucharistic Prayer, in which the entirety of our life is defined in relation to the triune God.

The dialogue continues, pushing us on to give thanks, to offer Eucharist, and we respond with the rather strange phrase, "It is right and just." To understand this acclamation, it is helpful to turn to Thomas Aquinas's own account of religion as justice. For Aquinas, religion is not simply a series of defined practices and beliefs related to God. Religion is a moral virtue, an act of justice in which human beings assume their proper status before God and one another as worshippers. He writes:

> Religion is neither a theological nor an intellectual, but a moral virtue, since it is a part of justice, and observes a mean, not in the passions, but in actions directed to God, by establishing a kind of equality in them. And when I say *equality*, I do not mean absolute equality, because it is not possible to pay God as much as we owe Him, but equality in consideration of man's ability [*humanae facultatis*] and God's acceptance [*divinae acceptationis*].[25]

In some ways, "ability" is a too tepid of a translation. Aquinas is speaking about how the act of worship, of religion, is a dedication of all our faculties, our capacities, our powers, to God. And this action is just, not simply because *we* perform it. Instead, God accepts our worship, finds it worthy, an esteeming deed of love that is ultimately sanctifying of our humanity. All of our virtues, our desires, and our capacities as human beings are taken up in worship and accepted as a worthy sacrifice before the living God.

Thus, the dialogue of the Eucharistic Prayer already establishes the human vocation to worship, to praise, to dedicating heart, mind, and soul to the God who first loved us. The Eucharist is not an escaping from life's difficulties, a movement toward the sacred that takes us away from the more mundane tasks of parenting, teaching, and study. Instead, it is an act of justice in which we bring all of ourselves before the living God, allowing our faculties of memory, understanding, and will to be offered to God. *It is right and just.*

Thanksgiving. Human beings seek to remember. Each year at football games at the University of Notre Dame, some historical team from the annals of Notre Dame football is brought back to be feted by the assembly of those gathered in the house that Rockne built. As fans, we meditate over the history of our program, waiting for that day when the glories of the past will become our present. We assume our vocation as Notre Dame fans not simply by attending a Saturday game but by immersing ourselves in the memories of that which has come before us.

Of course, college football (despite the sometimes sacral language used to speak about it) is simply a game. But the very same human need to remember, to give thanks for that which has been our past, is present in the Eucharistic Prayer of the church. In fact, through offering this prayer, we take up our vocation to give thanks and praise through the church's memory. The Thanksgiving or preface recalls the whole work of salvation, which makes the Eucharist possible in the first place. The preface focuses our attention upon one or two mysteries that illuminate the Christian life.

In Lent, we gave thanks in the preface for a season of fasting, almsgiving, and prayer. In Easter, we give thanks that the light of the resurrection has shattered the darkness of the old order with paschal joy. In Ordinary Time, we give thanks for specific aspects of salvation: our experience of God's care in our lives, the creation of humanity, and of course, Jesus Christ himself. These images, these ecclesial ruminations upon the triune God's action in history, enable our gratitude to assume a specific form.

This practice of remembering, of giving thanks for the mysteries of God revealed in Christ's life, death, and resurrection, is essential to our vocation as Christians. Immersed in the vicissitudes of time, we cannot always perceive how God acts in our history. Left to our own imagining, our own way of interpreting reality, we may grow forgetful that our existence is first and foremost a gift from God, a life being created and re-created by the Lord of history. We may gaze into the darker moments of our lives, those times in which the bitterness of tears and pain became our bread, and wonder where God was. The Christian answer is not a banal serenity. The Christian constantly must immerse him or herself in the eucharistic memory of the church so that we may begin to perceive the pedagogy of God, who continues to enter into salvation history through our lives. A couple who experiences the pain of infertility turns to the memory of the cross, to the self-gift that the God-Man offered even in the midst of human violence. Such remembering opens up a capacity in the couple, a love that they did not even know was possible. Likewise, we turn in gratitude to the creation of the world, remembering this deed of love. We remember the gift of creation in the eucharistic preface precisely because our perception needs to be slowly attuned to recognize the world as a gift to be received, and then offered again in love. The Christian who gives thanks on a regular basis in the Eucharistic Prayer develops a pattern of remembering God's marvelous deeds. We meditate upon the salvific action of the triune God, and we adopt the practice of expecting this God to continue to act in the concrete reality of our lives. We develop a discerning pattern of life through the art of eucharistic memory; an expectation that here and now, the Father, the Son, and the Spirit act. In this remembering, we practice seeing reality as it really is: a participation in God's marvelous plan of salvation.

This practice of thanksgiving infuses itself into the entirety of Christian practice. Take, for example, the practice of fasting on Fridays throughout the year. Such a practice has been retrieved by many of those involved in the new evangelization, including myself. Those of us, who cease eating meat, abstaining from specific foods on Fridays, are not seeking to return to the preconciliar era. Instead, through hunger, through abstaining from meat, we hope to embody the living memory of Christ's death and resurrection. We proclaim through our bodies the reality of Christ's death and resurrection, one that even now in this moment, influences every facet of our being. The thanksgiving of the Eucharistic Prayer as an act of memory, a joyful proclamation that Christ has indeed risen from the dead and begun the transformation of all creation, spills over into practices of rest on the Sabbath, of remembering the saints' days in our home, of keeping Lent and celebrating Easter. A pattern of life, of remembering Christ's gift of love, is implicit in the eucharistic praying of the church.

Sanctus. Following the preface, the whole congregation sings the acclamation (or *Sanctus*). This vital part of the Eucharistic Prayer is to be sung, the voices of the assembly joining with the heavenly hosts as described in the book of Isaiah. In discussing the theological implications of this liturgical practice, Bryan Spinks writes:

> For in Christian theology, the glory of God was revealed in Christ whose love and grace is revealed in the eucharistic feast. In Christ the space of heaven and the region of the earth are united. In the eucharist the worshipper enters heaven through Christ, and is represented by our true High Priest. Here time and eternity intersect and become one, and this world and the world to come elide. The words of the sanctus, whether said quietly, sung to a solemn but simple Gregorian chant, or to an elaborate polyphonic setting, can give the worshipper that glimpse of eternity which Isaiah experienced.[26]

The *Sanctus* orients Christian worship toward the union of heaven and earth, the in-breaking of eternal life in the here and now of this community's eucharistic offering. For heaven and earth are filled with the splendor and glory of the triune God. And the one who comes in the name of the Lord is Jesus Christ, the Word made flesh whose eucharistic presence dwells with the church through the ages. In the Eucharistic Prayer, we experience a foretaste of the heavenly vocation shared by the communion of saints and the angels. We experience glory through sensible signs: incense rising to the heavenly places; the illumination of the stained glass windows; the beauty of sung voices echoing throughout the church.

The practice of singing the *Sanctus* generates a pivotal insight regarding Christian vocation. My students often make the mistake of dismissing the quotidian reality of the present as the domain of God's action. They seek to turn to Catholic practice as an escape from the world, hoping that heaven will be better than this present age. In the process, they fail to perceive that in-breaking of divine life, which even now, can be glimpsed through sacramental signs. They await God's call as some foreign voice, which will resound in the interior silence of their heads, as an implanted vision from heaven. The singing of the *Sanctus* radically interrupts these assumptions. In the Eucharistic Prayer we experience the intersection of heaven and earth, of grace and nature, of sign and reality. We take up an expectant posture through the human voice lifted up in song that Jesus Christ is still coming.

Is not the wisdom of the liturgical practice of the *Sanctus* the very basis of the entire sacramental life of the church? Take, for example, the liturgical rites for the sacrament of marriage. In the Preface of Option B for the Celebration of Marriage, the church prays:

> It is truly right and just, our duty and our salvation,
> always and everywhere to give you thanks,
> Lord, holy Father, almighty and eternal God,
> through Christ our Lord.
> For in him you have made a new covenant with your people,
> so that, as you have redeemed man and woman
> by the mystery of Christ's Death and Resurrection,
> so in Christ you might make them partakers of divine nature
> and joint heirs with him of heavenly glory.
>
> In the union of husband and wife
> you give a sign of Christ's loving gift of grace,
> so that the Sacrament we celebrate might draw us back more deeply
>   into the wondrous design of your love.

The celebration of the sacrament of marriage is no mere ceremony, composed of the couple's desires and wishes for expressing their individual love together. Marriage is an eschatological sacrament, providing the church with an image of divine love, which draws us back to the eternal love of the Father. The couple's marriage liturgy does not cease at the conclusion of the hour- long rite. It continues into the present as the couple's deeper immersion into the art of self-giving love transforms them into increasingly authentic signs of God's love for the world. The quotidian nature of married life, of taking out the trash, paying the bills, and changing a child's diaper, are not mere responsibilities but a liturgical offering of love in which humanity and divinity are joined together.

The practice of the *Sanctus* shapes our vision to perceive this same eschatological, in-breaking of divine love possible in the entirety of Christian life. Our relationships, the concrete historical reality that we abide within, are those places where the eucharistic logic of the church unfolds; where heaven and earth wed in the poverty of visible signs. This vision of the *Sanctus*, of the eternal liturgy of praise, is essential to a robust theology of vocation for the new evangelization. As we practice the *Sanctus*, our vision is reconfigured to see the eschatological possibilities of the entire created order. We need not escape the world, to treat the visible signs of the liturgy as sacred moments that take us out of our present day lives and give us a taste of a world without sighs and sorrows. For our practice of liturgical prayer joins in an eternal liturgy, which is not our own, but is that of the angels and saints. Even now, as I sit in my office and engage in the work of being a professor, Christ comes again and again to my door in the student in need, in the co-worker experiencing sorrow, and in the gentle love I show in writing a book review. The liturgy of the world requires me to give of myself completely as an offering of praise to the Father for the transfiguration of the world.[27] The sensible signs employed in the church's eucharistic worship provide for me an authentic vision of that divine reality of love, even now coming into existence. The practice of praying the *Sanctus* in the eucharistic rites of the church gradually forms me in the art of expecting God's presence.

Epiclesis. In the Eucharistic Prayer, the epiclesis is that calling down of the Holy Spirit upon the bread and wine that these gifts formed by human hands might become *for us* Christ's Body and Blood. Recently, while watching a friend's child learn the names of his parents I had an insight into the wisdom of the consecratory epiclesis in the Roman Rite.[28] As any parent knows, as soon as young children learn to speak, they begin to call out "mom" and "dad" with persistent regularity. They delight in saying the name, of perceiving how their speech, can begin to influence the world around them. A world of possibilities open up as the child gains further capacity in speaking, now able to ask for what he or she wants. The child can express gratitude; to give thanks for all that he or she has received through the generous love of good parents.

In the same way, we, the church, those still learning the doxological speech of the kingdom, call down the Spirit to transform gifts of bread and wine (as well as the assembly later in the prayer).[29] We are learning a way of speaking, of transforming reality through human words knit into God's own grammar of love. In fact, there is a playful irony to eucharistic praying. We give thanks to God through the capacity of human speech, a gift bestowed by God in the first place. We present bread and wine upon the altar, knowing that wheat and grapes are gifts from that created order lavishly bestowed by God. Even our capacity to gather as the church, to praise and adore the living God through the liturgical rites of the church, is a gift received from the triune God. All that we offer to God is a gift.

The practice of praying the epiclesis embodies wisdom essential for the vocation of the church as the Body of Christ, as well as the individual Christian knit into the life of the church. Yves Congar, arguing for the epicletic nature of the church's very existence, writes:

> the part played by an intervention of the Holy Spirit and by an epi-
> clesis is to affirm that neither the "earthly means" nor the institution
> of the Church produces these [*participation in the events of salvation*]
> by themselves. What we have here is an absolutely supernatural work
> that is both divine and deifying. The Church can be sure that God works
> in it, but, because it is God and not the Church that is the principle of
> this holy activity, the Church has to pray earnestly for his intervention
> as a grace.[30]

The institution of the church acts in the world, it offers Eucharist, not because it has earned this gift through its own merits. The Eucharist, the church's mission to the world comes as total gift from the Spirit: "Under the Spirit's breath, the Word becomes our word: a word which comes closest to the truth when it wells forth in the very fissures of our discourses or murmurs in a hymn of silence. . . . The Spirit is the agent of this *enflesh-ment of the word*."[31] The church can consecrate, can offer Eucharist, can transform reality not because of the holiness of the ministers, because of the innate poetry of her rites, because of the stellar quality of her members. The capacity to pray the Eucharistic Prayer as Christ's own prayer of love offered to the Father is a gift received from the Spirit. The church can never be the community of the smug and the self-secure, precisely because our identity is not our own but received as a gift from the Spirit.

Those who practice praying the epiclesis in the rites of the church must learn to embody this wisdom in a way of life. It is the responsibility of each individual that attends the eucharistic liturgy and offers the Eucharistic Prayer to come to a deeper awareness of the epicletic nature of our histories—both within the darkness of our sins and the light of life. The Spirit who dwelt upon the waters of creation, who spoke through the prophets, who was breathed forth upon the apostles, descends upon our histories. We are gifted, yet we need to look honestly upon such gifts, acknowledging them not as something for which we alone are responsible.

The discernment of spirits, proposed by McIntosh, enacted in the Eucharistic Prayer, necessitates a self-knowledge that recognizes our tendency to grow forgetful of the Spirit-filled quality to our lives. We do not create ourselves, our gifts and talents are not ours alone. The project of vocational discernment is not simply about *me*, about what *I* plan on doing with the remainder of my days. Discernment necessarily includes allowing that same Spirit that transforms bread into Body and wine into Blood to descend upon my gifts and weaknesses. My ability to teach and to write is not my own alone but a gift from the Spirit who seeks to dwell in the drama of the classroom, in the mutilated words that I compose. Likewise, the very same Spirit seeks to heal the wounds of that sin of pride; one that manifests itself in my own desire to control my students' thoughts, to reorder the world according to the logic I have constructed. This latter, darker side of our giftedness, is something that we must constantly remember. The gift of a child, of becoming a parent, can easily descend into a desire to re-create ourselves in the life of this child, to form them in our own image and likeness. The gift of falling in love can devolve into the art of manipulation, of seeking to force another human being into my limited expectations and desires for his or her flourishing. Nonetheless, the Spirit dwells even here, in these weaknesses, in the wounds of sin that mark our memories and wills.

These gifts, these weaknesses, are all that we have. It is what we offer to the community when we come forth to the Eucharist. Yet, even the smallness of this gift, its mixed quality, this offering of a wounded self that takes place in every Eucharist is indispensable. As Rowan Williams writes:

> My charism, the gift given me to give to the community, is my *self*, ultimately; my story given back, to give me a place in the net of exchange, the web of gifts, which is Christ's church. My self is to be given away in love, not because it is worthless, but because it is supremely precious, given to me by the hand of God as he returns my memory. Out of my story, the Spirit of the risen Jesus constitutes my present possibilities of understanding, compassion, and self-sharing. My identity as lover in the community is uniquely coloured by the loves in which I have already struggled, failed, learned, repented: they are the reason for my present love being in this "key" or "mode" rather than that, the irreducible particularity of my gift.[32]

In the church's commitment to the new evangelization, to welcoming back those who have ceased to participate in our communion of love, nothing is more important than remembering the epicletic quality of our lives. We become a eucharistic people not because we have made ourselves entirely pure through the quality of our efforts. The God who is gift continues to send down that Spirit of gratitude upon the poverty of bread and wine, upon the poverty of our histories and desires, forming us again and again in the art of self-giving love. The Christian who practices the eucharistic epiclesis asks that this same Spirit descend into all the cracks and crevices of the human heart transforming it into the completeness of eucharistic love.

Institution Narrative or Consecration. After the epiclesis in the Roman Rite, the Eucharistic Prayer then moves toward the institution narrative, recalling that night when Christ supped with his disciples in the shadow of the cross. Most likely, the introduction of the institution narrative into the Eucharistic Prayer served a catechetical purpose, seeking to communicate the precise meaning of the liturgical action being celebrated.[33] Still, in the contemporary theology of the Roman Rite, the institution narrative is understood as a consecratory prayer, making Christ present through the power of the Spirit: "In the *institution narrative,* the power of the words and the action of Christ, and the power of the Holy Spirit, make sacramentally present under the species of bread and wine Christ's body and blood, his sacrifice offered on the cross for all."[34] How can we properly understand the practice of praying the institution narrative, and what relationship does such prayer have to vocation?

In his posthumous mystagogical text, *The Eucharist: Sacrament of the Kingdom,* Alexander Schmemann provides a theological account of the institution narrative, fruitful for vocation. He writes:

> "He loved them to the end" (John 13:1). In the eucharistic experience and in the gospels the last supper is the *end* (τέλος), i.e., the completion, the crowning, the fulfillment of Christ's love, which constitutes the essence of all of his ministry, preaching, miracles, and through which he now gives himself up, as love itself. From the opening words, "I have earnestly desired to eat this passover with you" (Luke 22:15), to the exit to the garden of Gethsemane, everything at the last supper—the washing of the feet, the distribution of the bread and the cup, the last discourse—is not only concerned with love, but is *Love itself.* And thus the last supper is the τέλος, the completion, the fulfillment of the *end,* for it is the manifestation of that kingdom of love, for the sake of which the world was created and in which it has its τέλος, its fulfillment. Through love God created the world. Through love he did not abandon it when it fell into sin and death. Through love he sent his only-begotten Son, his Love, into the world. And now, at this table,

he manifests and grants this love as his kingdom, and his kingdom as "abiding" in love: "As the Father has loved me, so have I loved you; *abide in my love*" (John 15:9).[35]

The institution narrative consecrates bread and wine not because they are magic words, inviting us into a reenactment of the Last Supper. These words are a synecdoche, a part for the whole that remembers the radical claim that God is love unto the end. All of Christ's life was an "instituting narrative" in which death was defeated through the love of God, who descended into the human condition as one of us. God who from the very beginning of time entered into a sacrificial relationship of creating and redeeming humanity. And in the institution narrative, we remember that this very same triune God continues to pour himself out in the fullness of love *in this place, in this time, on this holy table, in this body of believers.*

This narrative of divine love remains for us *the* instituting narrative, one that radically forms the identity of Christians; we who seek to imitate the radical self-gift of Christ in the unfolding of our lives in time and space. There are other narratives. Often, they disfigure our identities. There is that narrative that we can only be considered beautiful when measured against the impossible standards of photoshopped models on covers of magazines. There is that narrative that success in life is dependent upon the largesse of our salary. There is that narrative that proclaims that we as human beings are in control of life, can judge whether or not a creature is truly human, and thus disposable according to our technological, political, and economic possibilities. There is that narrative that states violence is the only way to be secure. All such narratives shatter under the weight of the institution narrative. Practicing the institution narrative in our lives means that we must constantly allow the narrative of divine love to critique all other assumptions we have regarding what it means to be fully human. Our praying of this narrative reveals the radical vocation we have to self-gift.

The God of love, Jesus Christ, comes to dwell among us in the Eucharistic Prayer of the church. The desire to treat this part of the Eucharistic Prayer as more than "magic words" does not mean that we are to dismiss the reality that Christ becomes fully present in bread-once-bread and wine-once-wine. The doctrine of transubstantiation, our belief that the substance (the reality) of the Eucharist is transformed into the Body and Blood of Christ, while the accidents (the physical properties) remain, is pivotal to the eucharistic praying of the church. Some might object that this doctrine is too philosophical, too complex, too exact to have anything to do with developing a discerning pattern of life. Joseph Ratzinger disagrees. He writes:

When material things are taken into our body as nourishment, or for that matter whenever any material becomes part of a living organism, it remains the same, and yet as part of a new whole it is itself changed. Something similar happens here. The Lord takes possession of the bread and the wine; he lifts them up, as it were, out of the setting of their normal existence into a new order; even if, from a purely physical point of view, they remain the same, they have become profoundly different.[36]

In this teaching of the church, a deeper eucharistic wisdom is revealed to the Christian. Our lives, reality itself as taken up in the eucharistic praying of the church also operate in an entirely distinct order: "this capacity things have for being transformed makes us more aware that the world itself can be transformed, that it will one day as a whole be the New Jerusalem, the Temple, vessel of the presence of God."[37] Indeed, much of human life for the Christian might look exactly the same as those who do not profess that Jesus Christ has defeated death by his death. We both have families, we both participate in careers, we both give ourselves over to causes that transcend our city or nation. The distinction is that for the Christian, such matter, even that touched by unbelievers, is being transformed into the fullness of the presence of God. Matter is being divinized.

This claim is an act of faith. Often, our senses do not perceive anything remarkable about family life, about a particular act of love to someone in need. We may grow in despair, abiding in a created order in which justice and love seem to have no effect upon the hardness of the human heart. Yet, to the one formed in eucharistic faith, we can perceive the possibility of the transfiguration of all reality. The Body and Blood of Christ, the eucharistic presence dwelling in our churches, is a constant reminder that the physical world, what we can see and taste and smell, is being slowly transformed through that very real, spiritual reality of God's love.

Eucharistic adoration, then, is not necessarily a problematic development in ecclesial practice. Rather, it is the extension of eucharistic gratitude, of that instituting narrative of eucharistic love into the concrete and quotidian life of the church. As Nathan Mitchell writes, "As both liturgical action and permanent sacrament, the eucharist has led believers to the conviction that the Lord continues to be available, present, interested in the variegated textures of human life and history. The story, the action, and the mystery continue to unfold."[38] We practice the institution narrative within the form of our life when we begin to perceive that reality itself is forever changed, transformed, in light of Christ's resurrection. Eucharistic adoration is a concrete practice, which re-orders our hearts to the presence of the God who seeks to incarnate his narrative into our lives.

Anamnesis and Oblation. Following the memorial acclamation, the second part of the Eucharistic Prayer commences. Quoting from the Eucharistic Prayer I, the Roman Canon:

> Therefore, O Lord,
> as we celebrate the memorial of the blessed Passion,
> the Resurrection from the dead,
> and the glorious Ascension into heaven
> of Christ, your Son, our Lord,
> we, your servants and your holy people,
> offer to your glorious majesty
> from the gifts that you have given us,
> this pure victim,
> this holy victim,
> this spotless victim,
> the holy Bread of eternal life
> and the Chalice of everlasting salvation.
>
> Be pleased to look upon these offerings
> with a serene and kindly countenance,
> and to accept them,
> as once you were pleased to accept
> the gifts of your servant Abel the just,
> the sacrifice of Abraham, our father in faith,
> and the offering of your high priest Melchizidek,
> a holy sacrifice, a spotless victim.
>
> In humble prayer we ask you, almighty God:
> command that these gifts be born
> by the hands of your holy Angel
> to your altar on high
> in the sight of your divine majesty,
> so that all of us, who through this participation at the altar
> receive the most holy Body and Blood of your Son,
> may be filled with every grace and heavenly blessing.

To those who are novices in Eucharistic Prayer structures, there is a kind of strangeness to this portion of the prayer. After all, have we not been remembering God's great deeds of salvation throughout the Eucharistic Prayer?

In his recent book on the Eucharist, John Laurance, S.J., provides a sound interpretation of the anamnesis (the church's celebration of the paschal mystery of Christ) and oblation (the offering of the eucharistic victim by the church, as well as the offering of each believer). He writes:

> What, then, Christians give thanks for in the church's eucharistic prayer is Jesus Christ in his life, death, and resurrection as the fullness of the Father's self-gift, a gift realized throughout all creation but made present to believers especially through their own self-offering. . . . Just as the Father gave himself fully to the incarnate Son, and to all humanity in him, through the Son's self-giving on the cross to the Father, so does the Son ask us to let him continue, now and through our self-offering in him, to give himself both to the Father and to us.[39]

We remember the fullness of the Son's offering to the Father, his taking up of humanity into divine life, and we offer this gift back to the Father as an act of love. Like with the epiclesis, we are offering to the Father a gift that we have already received from him in the Son. The triune God bestows to us the very gift that we offer up, a spotless Victim who loved unto the end.

The language of victim, of sacrifice, may be a bit terrifying for us. After all, it places us face-to-face with the violence of the cross, the violence that we continue to perpetuate when we gossip as a way of tearing down the neighbor, when we delight in the suffering of others. Yet, this violence is rendered mute. Christ is the Passover Victim, who has conquered death through emptying himself into the totality of love. This offering of total love, of self-gift, allows us to participate in that beatific life in which the violence of the cross has been bathed in resurrected light.

To receive the Body and Blood of Christ is then to perform a self-implicating act, one in which we are to become that peaceful, eucharistic offering for the salvation of the world. Eucharistic Prayer III asks God to "Look, we pray, upon the oblation of your Church and, recognizing the sacrificial Victim by whose death you willed to reconcile us to yourself, grant that we, who are nourished by the Body and Blood of your Son and filled with his Holy Spirit, may become one body, one spirit in Christ." Our praying of the Eucharist is not a communion of an isolated individual with God. The offering that we are learning to make is that of the redeemed city, the peace of a humanity that lives according to the eucharistic logic of God. To perform this act of memory (the anamnesis), to make this offering (the oblation), necessitates a renewal of our entire lives according to the peace of the kingdom.

In a way, the eucharistic vocation of the Christian becomes most clear in the practice of anamnesis and oblation. The Christian does not need to establish some intimate union between liturgy and life through force of will, as if the two are separate spheres. The parish community that refuses to follow unjust laws against immigrants performs that eucharistic oblation, that offering of peace intrinsic to the kingdom in which all of humanity is to become one body and one Spirit in Christ. This deed of justice is an act of remembering, of embodying in time and space, the Lord's passion, resurrection, and ascension. A priest, who loves those in his parish (even the most challenging ones), is not simply being a decent pastor but continuing that eucharistic offering, which is to define his existence as one who acts in the person of Christ and the church. The catechist, who delights in recounting the narrative of salvation to junior high students as a balm for the pains and sorrows of early adolescence continues that eucharistic gift, which has become defining of her life. No part of our humanity is to be held back in the eucharistic remembering and offering of the church: "Character in all its manifestations; our habitual thoughts and actions, our interests and our work, our aims and our relationships, our everyday routine, are here to be unselfed and orientated towards eternity; made part of the eternal sacrifice which the created order offers in Christ to God."[40] Such work is not always easy. It requires a form of liturgical ascesis, of discipline, whereby we begin to view the entirety of our lives vis-à-vis the peaceful, eucharistic offering of Christ himself.[41] We know how difficult it is to love the political foe whose agenda seeks to deconstruct all that we hold dear, the co-worker who tears us down in secret, the terrorist who belches forth violence rather than peace. Love in such situations, the hard ones, is precisely the kind of formation that the Eucharist provides. Politics, art, the academic life, family, all that is most human are rich fields for eucharistic remembering and offering.

Intercessions. At the beginning of every practice of the Notre Dame Glee Club, we would offer our prayers for all those in need. We prayed for the sick in our midst (a common prayer in the middle of a South Bend winter), for those suffering from the effects of natural disasters, for a good time for those visiting campus over the weekend, for the football team's successful dismantling of that weekend's opponent. Such intercessions would quickly become a way of updating our fellow Brothers-in-Song about successes and failures in our lives. Other forms of prayer rarely were used in the context of the Glee Club, and for this reason, we become experts at tuning out the deepest desires, the deepest sorrows, the deepest joys of one another.

Within the Eucharistic Prayer, we begin to offer intercession for the church and the world. In our humanity, there is a need to call out to God, to ask for intercession in our lives. The eucharistic liturgy offers two major times for such intercession: the universal prayer of the church following the Creed and in the Eucharistic Prayer proper. Let us attend to the first, so that we might understand more deeply how the intercessions of the Eucharistic Prayer reveal a discerning pattern of life.

The Liturgy of the Word concludes with the universal prayer of the church. In this prayer, all of us gathered exercise our baptismal priesthood. Because Jesus Christ is our high priest, every word that we utter is offered to the Father by the Son. God listens to the words that we speak. And though we may never fully see the fruit of our prayers, it does not mean that God does not hear us. In fact, intercessory prayer does not simply change the world, it may even change us. This is a difficult truth to learn. We have undoubtedly offered prayers that have gone unanswered. Some of us have prayed that the ones we love most would not die, and yet we found ourselves at the funeral months later. As the *Catechism of the Catholic Church* (CCC) notes regarding this prayer, "The prayer of Jesus makes Christian prayer an efficacious petition. He is its model, he prays in us and with us. Since the heart of the Son seeks only what pleases the Father, how could the prayer of the children of adoption be centered on the gifts rather than the Giver?" (CCC 2740). In the universal prayer of the church, we pray that God's will be done throughout the world, and we are slowly attuned to recognize what the Father's will is, through union with the Son.

The practice of intercessory prayer takes on further meaning in the context of eucharistic praying. We have proclaimed God's wondrous deeds in history; we have opened our imaginations to the eternal reality in-breaking into the present; we have asked that the Spirit descend upon us; we have remembered that love alone is the meaning of all existence, and we have made a commitment to offer the living God through the eucharistic transformation of our bodies. Then, we assume our vocations to intercede for the church and the world, for the renewal of humankind. Jean Corbon writes:

> The intercessions . . . bring the power of this eucharistic Pentecost
> to bear on everything that we offer to the Father. In union with Christ
> we stand before the face of the Father and intercede for all. . . . May
> the Holy Spirit come! He who is "the place of the saints" expands his
> presence through our intercessions. The church, in virginal faith, ex-
> periences with him the gestation of the world . . . she consents to be
> the new tomb wherein is laid the human race that has been wounded

by death. In its intercession, that is, in its epiclesis, the church gives
her freest and most detached consent to the life-giving Spirit. In the
interceding church human weakness becomes the living locus in which
the power of God acts . . . the sin of men becomes the crack through
which healing and the fullness of divine grace come to them.[42]

The practice of intercessory prayer in a eucharistic context is an extension of the epiclesis, a realization of the vocation of all those knit into
the baptismal life of the church to ask for the Spirit to descend upon the
vicissitudes of history. We pray for the communion of the whole church,
visible and invisible.

The vocation of the Christian is to spiritually intercede before the Father,
through Jesus Christ, for the entire world. In some ways, this is one of the
most difficult facets of eucharistic practice to retrieve. Prayer works not
through manipulating God to obtain what we desire. It works because it
sanctifies the created order, lifting up all the sorrows and the joys of human
life to the Father. My undergraduates all desire to change the world through
service, commitment to the poor, and engagement in a job that they love,
but they are reticent to admit that spiritual gifts of love, prayer, silence, and
solitude change creation. Our vocation as Christians is not simply to feed
the poor, to enact new just laws, but also to love the poor, to pray for them,
to ask that the Spirit will descend upon those most in need. We pray for the
pope and the bishop precisely because our responsibility as citizens of the
church is not simply to serve on the parish council, to offer our insight into
better financial and governmental structures for the church, but to pray
that the Spirit of the Father and the Son will descend upon our leadership,
forming them into the image of Jesus Christ, who descends into the depths
of love. The wounds and sorrows of human life are to be lifted up in the
silence of prayer.

Of course, such intercession does commit us to action. It makes no
sense for us to pray for peace within the world while we promote violence
in the workplace through gossip and scandal. It is illogical to pray for our
governmental leaders, only to disengage entirely from the political sphere,
to recognize our responsibility to promote justice at home and abroad. It is
strange to pray for the pope, only to rip him apart in public settings as we
take up a hermeneutics of suspicion that poisons our soul. Christians must
practice the art of interceding through prayers that take flesh in our bodies
given over in love to the world. The only rational response of the Christian
who recognizes the power of intercession is to assume the virtue of lov-
ing hospitality. We must become like the God who welcomes our prayers

by opening our homes, our classrooms, our studios, and every part of our world and interior life to all those who come to us seeking a communion, a love they cannot yet name. Intercessory prayer does not simply change the world; rather it changes us to love the world aright. Evelyn Underhill writes:

> So the Great Intercession, placed at the very heart of the Eucharist, to check as it were the forth rush of the soul towards God, reminds us that Christianity is not a religion of escape; that is accepts the full burden, fret and responsibility of humanity, does not evade it. The Christian communicant goes to the altar as a member of the family; not as one who has contracted out of the family life. He goes to offer himself to that God, who in Christ reconciled the world to Himself. Intercession . . . embraces the whole world in its scope, not only the respectable but the disgraceful. The confusions, sins, and cruelties; the people and policies that we should prefer to forget; the horrors, the failures, the short ends. All these it can, by mysterious power of sacrifice, lift up and reconcile to God.[43]

Intercession is the Christian practice embodied in the eucharistic offering that slowly forms us to love, to pray for those we despise and those who are not yet in union with us. It ensures that we do not escape the world, into our own private image of what constitutes the church of the redeemed. Laity and clerics who grasp and seize power, politicians who manipulate laws for their own benefit: we must love and ask for the presence of the Spirit even on these.

Doxology. The Eucharistic Prayer then concludes with the doxology, the great hymn of praise to the triune God: "Through him, and with him, and in him, O God, almighty Father, in the unity of the Holy Spirit, all glory and honor is yours, for ever and ever." The Great Amen resounds, and then silence falls over the assembly. The doxology, the concluding note of the Eucharistic Prayer, is a summary of all that we have prayed thus far. As has been said throughout this mystagogical treatment of the discerning pattern of life made possible through eucharistic praying, our lives are not our own. They are inscribed in a gift already received from the God who created the world and redeemed it through his Son Jesus Christ, and even now renews our hearts through the power of the Spirit. Our ability to pray and to offer a sacrifice of love is made possible only through this God.

From a theological perspective, what is most remarkable about the doxology is that it *concludes* a rather long prayer. The human voice, given over to speech, bestows itself to laudatory song once more, and then to silence. In the doxology, we move from the hustle and bustle of the economy of the salvation to the interior silence of the mystery of the triune God, who is absolute self-gift.[44] Indeed, there is a wisdom inscribed in this movement toward doxological silence. Certainly, if there is one form of communication, which our present day liturgies often lack, it is that of silent contemplation before the mystery of God. But such contemplation is not simply reserved to the eucharistic rites of the church; after all, the Eucharistic Prayer ends, it does not continue on forever. Eucharistic praying calls the Christian forth to learn the art of contemplation, "a silent prayer which takes place in recollection in the secret of the heart, and is directly ordered to union with God."[45]

The eucharistic vocation of the Christian finds its end not in more prayer, in ever more beautiful speech but in the silence of total love. The eucharistic praying of the church manifests to each Christian that we are called to nothing less than contemplative union with God. Our vocation will be the total gift of ourselves, of our memories, our imaginations, and our will to the mystery of divine love. This total participation in the divine life, reserved for the eternal Sabbath, is a perfect union of knowledge and love: "there we shall be at leisure and will see, we shall see and will love and we shall love and will praise."[46] The entirety of our being, the whole city of humanity, will become a eucharistic offering of praise. We will become doxological.

The eucharistic life of the church, our practice of praying the doxology and then concluding with silence, bestows to us an image of who *we* are to become: the perfection of praise. The entirety of those gathered in our parish, those who participate in the Eucharistic Prayer of the church, whose virtues seem to be lacking for us, are destined for a doxological existence, for the beatific vision. The conclusion of the Eucharistic Prayer provides for us an image of the kind of humility that is required if we are to partake in this sort of eucharistic communion, if we are to recognize that all humanity is to be redeemed through the rites of the church. In Flannery O'Connor's "Revelation," Mrs. Turpin, adept at reordering the world according to her own image and likeness, comes to a doxological, prophetic vision of what our union into God will involve:

> A visionary light settled in her eyes. She saw the streak as a vast swinging bridge extending upward from the earth through a field of living fire. Upon it a vast horde of souls were rumbling toward heaven. There were whole companies of white-trash, clean for the first time in their lives, and bands of black niggers in white robes, and battalions of

> freaks and lunatics shouting and clapping and leaping like frogs. And
> bringing up the end of the procession was a tribe of people whom she
> recognized at once as those who, like herself and Claud, had a little of
> everything and the God-given wit to use it right. She learned forward
> to observe them closer. They were marching behind the others with
> great dignity, accountable as they had always been for good order and
> common sense and respectable behavior. They alone were on key. Yet,
> she could see by their shocked and altered faces that even their virtues
> were being burned away.[47]

Our doxological union with the triune God comes with a cost. It comes with
the cost of recognizing that our eucharistic praying obligates us to a way
of life in which even our virtues, our gifts, and all that which we perceive
as most worthy in us must be burned away through divine love. Our destiny as Christians, our vocation is nothing less than union into God. Such a
union does not erase difference but it does require that we begin to see that
the only virtue, the only laudatory gift that we bring to the Father, is the
gift of our whole selves offered to the consuming fire of the triune God's
redemptive love.

Attending to the discerning pattern of life implicit in the Eucharistic
Prayer results in a reconsideration of the very question of vocation, of that
human need to know how we might contribute to the reign of God. The question is not simply what we are to do with our lives but rather what our lives
are to become. The vocation of each Christian, whether lay or ordained, is
eucharistic love. In the practice of praying this prayer, we develop a pattern
of life in which our memory is turned over to the practice of giving thanks
to the triune God for the redemption of humanity accomplished in Jesus
Christ, a narrative that is still being played out here in the concrete details
of our lives. We join with the heavenly hosts in that liturgy of eternal praise,
which calls for us to gaze upon the quotidian not as devoid of God's presence
but as the bodily and historical reality, which is being taken up into the eucharistic love of God. We ask for the Spirit to descend upon gifts of bread
and wine, upon the gifts of our lives, so that our identity might be infused
with the salvific Spirit of the living God. We pray the institution narrative
as manifesting the fullness of God's love, a love that interrupts every other
narrative we have regarding human fulfillment; we dwell in the abiding
eucharistic love of God, even when we cannot perceive it. We remember
the glorious deeds of Christ, and we offer these very gifts made present on

the altar to God; in the process, we offer ourselves, asking that God might transform every part of our being into a living sacrifice. We stand before the Father, through Christ and the power of the Spirit, interceding before the world, daring to pray that God's love might descend upon even the darkest places of human history. And lastly, we enter into the doxological grammar of the church's prayer, seeking a contemplative union with the triune God.

The Eucharistic Prayer offers a discerning pattern of life, one intrinsic to that new evangelization that seeks to transfigure society, culture, and our individual lives according to the prodigal logic of the Gospel. Each time we pray this prayer, we need not think through every part. If performed well, eucharistic praying becomes a habit, a disposition, and a liturgical practice that we engage in without conscious thought. But, if we begin to conceive of eucharistic praying as central to Christian practice, if we allow the logic of this prayer to infiltrate into every corner of our lives, we may discover that we begin to undertake vocational discernment in light of eucharistic wisdom. The Christian, whose vocation becomes eucharistic, will proclaim the Gospel not merely in word but in that eucharistic living, which will inevitably invite others to *taste and see how good the Lord is* (Ps 34:8).

Rites of Return 5

In recent years Catholics have begun to feature a series of television advertisements, inviting those baptized Catholics absent from the assembly to "come home." The commercials laud the tradition of the church and the richness of the liturgical life embodied in its prayer. Likewise, they remind families that involvement in Catholic faith is healthy for the vitality of family life. But a question remains: what are such Catholics coming home to? Perhaps, the parish that one begins to attend celebrates a minimalistic liturgical rite, devoid of music, and with impoverished preaching. Perchance the parish is inhospitable to those newcomers, simply pretending that they do not exist (or gazing suspiciously upon them when they enter). Other parishes may treat Catholic faith not as something rich, transforming of human life, but as an obligation that we must sustain in the midst of secular forces beyond our control. Some who come home to the church seeking a sacrament of initiation for a child, are greeted not with a full bodied vision of the sacramental life of the church, but a series of rules and regulations regarding the sacrament, many of which are simply the local guidelines for *this* parish.

Why should we come home to this, one might ask? Indeed, pivotal to the work of new evangelization is a transformation of the entire life of the parish itself, including its liturgical rites. The joy of Catholic life, even in the midst of the sorrows of the world and the church's own tendency to sinfulness, should infuse the parish. Its members should embody that art of humble, self-giving love learned in the womb of the liturgical life of the church. In this chapter, we turn our attention to the parish. Relative to the new evangelization, I do not ask simply how one might get more people into the pews but instead seek to understand what sort of liturgical and sacramental life greets those returning. This chapter consists of three parts. In the first, I outline the liturgical disposition that must infuse all prayer within the parish, awareness that each liturgical rite is a "rite of return." In the second, I submit that the liturgical-sacramental life of the parish will evangelize when it is both beautiful and humanizing. Lastly, in what serves as a conclusion to this volume, I suggest that a renewed liturgical movement, one arising from lay communities operating together with parishes, may be a fruitful way of transforming parish life, capacitating it for the new evangelization.

Coming Home

As has been argued throughout this book, the heart of the new evangelization is a spiritual renewal of the entire life of the church, one that leads to the practice of self-giving love in the world. In the liturgical prayer of the church, we return each day to learn anew this art form. The praying of the Divine Office each morning invites the whole church, whether attending the Office or not, to return to the vocation of divine praise. A couple, absent from the church for years, approaches the minister seeking baptism for their newborn child, expressing an implicit desire for a salvation they do not fully comprehend. Lapsed Catholics return during the transitional rites of baptism and funerals, while those well practiced in Catholicism renew their commitment to a life conformed to the paschal mystery of Christ. The parish's Sunday Eucharist invites each member of the Body of Christ to remember once again our deepest identity as made in the image and likeness of God, a creature whose calling is love unto the end. All liturgical prayer—the whole sacramental life—is an invitation to return to that self-giving love, defining of Christian existence.

As the church explores what constitutes the new evangelization relative to the liturgical rites, the theme of return is pivotal. Too often the issue of return focuses solely upon inviting those Catholics back to the parish who have been away for some time. Such an approach, while indispensable to the new evangelization, is partial at best. If a Catholic returns only to discover a parish so smug, so sure of its holiness, believing that it has arrived at the summit of Christian charity, then the newly returned Catholic will depart once again.

The language of return must then be located in the very nature of liturgical prayer itself. The new evangelization is a spiritual renewal of the entire assembly; a realization that we are in the process of being re-created into the image and likeness of God, constantly returning to the font of ecclesial life. The process of returning, reorienting our existence back to the Father through the Son in the unity of the Holy Spirit is central to patristic liturgical theology. In his *Spirit of the Liturgy*, encapsulating this theological tradition, Joseph Ratzinger writes:

> The *exitus*, or rather God's free act of creation, is indeed ordered toward the *reditus,* but that does not now mean the rescinding of created being. . . . The creature, existing in its own right, comes home to itself, and this act is answer in freedom to God's love. It accepts creation from God as his offer of love, and thus ensues a dialogue of love, that wholly new kind of unity that love alone can create. The being of the other is not absorbed or abolished, but rather, in giving itself, it becomes fully itself. . . . This *reditus* is a "return," but it does not abolish creation; rather, it bestows its full and final perfection.[1]

In worship, we return a word of amorous dialogue to the God whose speech is love itself. And "returning" this word of love, we become our truest selves. The process of redemption is learning to speak true words of love in worship. Ratzinger writes:

> If "sacrifice" in its essence is simply returning to love and therefore divinization, worship now has a new aspect: the healing of wounded freedom, atonement, purification, deliverance from estrangement. The essence of worship, of sacrifice—the process of assimilation, of growth in love, and thus the way into freedom—remains unchanged. But now it assumes the aspect of healing, the loving transformation of broken freedom, of painful expiation.[2]

No Christian, until he or she enjoys God in eternal life, has fully returned to authentic creaturehood. We are pilgrims on the way toward the fullness of love and participating in the church's worship is our slow return to the authentic life of freedom made possible by divine love. Worship returns us to our identity as creatures made in the image and likeness of God.

What does it mean to say that human beings are made in the image and likeness of God? To an unsophisticated reader of the book of Genesis, one may imagine that human beings are physical copies of an anthropomorphic God, an interpretation that results in a rather impoverished understanding of both God and humanity alike. Attending to the text in Genesis, "And God said, 'Let us make man in our image, after our likeness. They shall rule the fish of the sea, the birds of the sky, the cattle, the whole earth, and all the creeping things that creep on earth.' And God created man in His image, in the image of God He created him; male and female He created them" (Gen 1:26-28). The language of image and likeness is related not to some interior disposition of human beings, an intellectual capacity that we possess. Instead, humanity is created in the image and likeness of God insofar as we are made to rule the created order. Such an interpretation of the text may evoke caution within us: is it not the case that our ruling over creation has resulted in ecological destruction, in the subjection of various peoples throughout the world? But, humanity's responsibility as "rulers of creation" must be understood within the broader context of the creation narrative. In Genesis, the Father creates out of sheer gift, through the salutary power of the Word and Spirit. The created order is not a chaotic nihilism, a world without meaning in which darkness lurks. At the heart of creation is the goodness of a God who has entered into relationship with the created order, forming creation as a meaningful gift of love.

Human beings are created in the image and likeness of *this God*, not a God who seeks to make us hired servants but rather desires to include us within the project of creation as gift. As Joseph Ratzinger writes, "the image of God . . . means that human persons are beings of word and of love, beings moving toward Another, oriented to giving themselves to the Other and only truly receiving themselves back in real self-giving."[3] To be created in the image and likeness of God situates human life in the outpouring of self-gift. The tragedy of the fall is that our act of disobedience is not against a tyrant, seeking to limit human freedom, but a God who desires to share divine life with us. Sin has led to a disfigurement of our status as created in the image and likeness of God; it is fall from gratitude into self-reliance:

> Here we can at once say that at the very heart of sin lies human beings' denial of their creatureliness, inasmuch as they refuse to accept the standard and the limitations that are implicit in it. They do not want to be creatures, do not want to be subject to a standard, do not want to be dependent. They consider their dependence on God's creative love to be an imposition from without. But that is what slavery is and from slavery one must free oneself. Thus human beings themselves want to be God. When they try this, everything is thrown topsy-turvy. The relationship of human beings to themselves is altered, as well as their relationship to others. The other is a hindrance, a rival, a threat to the person who wants to be God. The relationship with the other becomes one of mutual recrimination and struggle. . . . Human beings who consider dependence on the highest love as slavery and who try to deny the truth about themselves, which is their creatureliness, do not free themselves; they destroy truth and love. They do not make themselves gods, which in fact they cannot do, but rather caricatures, pseudo-gods, slaves of their own abilities, which then drag them down.[4]

We need not rely solely on the Genesis narrative to discover the consequences of human sin relative to our capacity for self-gift. We gossip and gripe about those we work with as a way of grasping a power that we do not have. We look with envy upon the gifts of others, complaining to God that our breakthrough, our moment in the spotlight has not yet arrived. We drink too much as a way of escaping from the sorrows of our lives, only to discover that the pain remains. We grow to hate our most difficult student because he or she does not bend the will to what we would hope. We refuse to accept compliments, yet secretly crave the moment in which we can receive the praise of others. We no longer look upon our spouse, our children with gratitude but see them as another obstacle in our lives, another relationship to submit to. We cease praying because we have come to believe that the source of our ministry, of our gifts, is not the lavishness of divine grace but our own special talent, *me and me alone.* Even the "advanced" Christian, one practiced in the art of self-giving love, is constantly at risk of this sin of pride, seeking to reorder the world not according to divine generosity but to one's own ingenuity.

Of course, what seemed like a tragedy within the fall became for the Christian the comedy of divine revelation when Jesus Christ, in the totality of his self-gift, revealed to us what it means to be created in the image and likeness of God. Continuing his explication of the creation account, Ratzinger writes:

> Christ is the new Adam, with whom humankind begins anew. The Son, who is by nature relationship and relatedness, reestablishes relationships. His arms, spread out on the cross, are an open invitation to relationship, which is continually offered to us. The cross, the place of his obedience, is the true tree of life. . . . From this tree there comes not the word of temptation but that of redeeming love, the word of obedience, which an obedient God himself used, thus offering us his obedience as a context for freedom. The cross is the tree of life, now become approachable. . . . Therefore the Eucharist, as the presence of the cross, is the abiding tree of life, which is ever in our midst and ever invites us to take the fruit of true life. . . . To receive it, to eat of the tree of life, thus means to receive the crucified Lord and consequently to accept the parameters of his life, his obedience, his "yes," the standard of our creatureliness.[5]

Through our initiation into the sacramental life of the church, we enter into the life of the Son and thus are re-created into the image and likeness of God.[6] Liturgical worship is an exercise in once again saying yes to God, offering the entirety of our being to the Father as an act of love. It is to stand before God as a creature, giving up our distorted view that we are the Creator. The full expression of our identity as created in the image and likeness of God is manifested in divine worship.

For this reason every liturgical action (at least in principle) becomes for the Christian a rite of return, a re-creation of our identities according to the image and likeness of God. When liturgical participants sign themselves with the cross, they mark their bodies as a space given over to the Father in love, entering into the primary relationship of obedient love defining of Christian existence. The genuflection of a single person passing before the Tabernacle manifests an offering of the body through ritual action to God, a sacramental enactment of God's very presence dwelling among us. Those who receive the anointing of the sick bestow the entirety of their being, including the pain of illness, to God, "the trustworthy companion or sheltering parent or stronger sibling or Good Shepherd or all powerful Lord who can accept our tears, bear our yearnings, withstand our anger—who only desires that we be real in our presence."[7] Gathering at the Sunday Eucharist, we interrupt the routine of the American weekend, reordering our desires according to the eucharistic logic of the church. In the act of singing within liturgical worship, our voices, our hearts, are lifted up to God; the violence of human speech, at times dedicated to coercion, reorients itself to the gift of divine praise. The liturgical prayer of the church reforms our speech, our action, placing us once again in that spirit of gratitude that defined the paradisiacal vocation of humanity.

Of course, liturgical prayer does not necessarily restore us to the image and likeness of God. Too often, such prayer is not offered from the wounded heart of a humanity seeking to be healed through divine love but from a smug sensibility that *we* are the proprietors, the owners of our own worship, and the perfectly converted. Eucharistic liturgies can become exercises in human power, occasions of worshipping ourselves, of drawing political and cultural lines where the Gospel requires the prodigal logic of the kingdom. I often pay attention to the way in which some eucharistic ministers establish hierarchies of order among each other; how liturgy committees treat the parish's Sunday Eucharist as the occasion for expressing their own private liturgical taste, exerting their will upon the assembly; how various communities within the parish establish an in-group and an out-group, deforming the liturgical rites of the church into the private gathering of the wealthy and the powerful. The problem, of course, is not the church's liturgical rites: it's us! We may distort the church's liturgy, treating it as an idol, an occasion for placing ourselves at the center of the cosmos. But even in the midst of our perverted desire to treat the liturgy as an idol of our own limited vision of the kingdom:

> God gives and forgives; he fore-gives and gives again. There is no calculable economy in this trinitarian discourse of love, to which creation is graciously admitted. There is only the gift and the restoration of the gift, the love that the gift declares, the motion of giving that is infinite, which comprehends every sacrifice made according to love, and which overcomes every sacrifice made for the sake of power.[8]

The church is the community of those seeking to become the image and likeness of God, the communion of those being healed to recognize how every moment of creation for those living in Christ is gift. Our identity as the church does not come from our own remarkable intelligence, the aesthetic virtues of our worship, the social consciousness that we inspire among our members, or the vitality of our assembly. It comes from the gift of a God, who slowly forms our speech to name the created order aright. The liturgical worshipper, even one committed to daily eucharistic worship, is constantly in need of being converted to this reality, of returning to God in love. All of us must learn to take up the speech of the poet George Herbert in his classic "Love (3)":

> Love bade me welcome: yet my soul drew back,
>   Guilty of dust and sin.
> But quick-eyed Love, observing me grow slack
>   From my first entrance in,
> Drew nearer to me, sweetly questioning,
>   If I lacked anything.
>
> A guest, I answered, worthy to be here:
>   Love said, You shall be he.
> I the unkind, ungrateful? Ah my dear,
>   I cannot look on thee.
> Love took my hand, and smiling did reply,
>   Who made the eyes but I?
>
> Truth Lord, but I have marred them: let my shame
>   Go where it doth deserve.
> And know you not, says Love, who bore the blame?
>   My dear, then I will serve.

You must sit down, says Love, and taste my meat:
So I did sit and eat.[9]

If a parish inhabits such a disposition, an awareness of gratitude that infuses the liturgical assembly, then the offering of hospitality, of welcome to those returning, will become a *habitus* of love. Our whole identity will become an offering of humble hospitality, whereby we welcome the recently returned not out of obligation but out of the depths of Christian charity, a continuation of the worshipful dialogue taken up in the church's rites. We are happy to welcome back those long absent, whether returning for a funeral, penance, a wedding, or a baptism, not merely to increase our numbers but because in their presence the Body of Christ is built up and the world transformed. The newly returned are fellow saints in the making. All of us gathered in the assembly are discovering again what it means to love as one made in the image and likeness of God within the curriculum of the church's prayer.

Liturgical Beauty that Humanizes

Thus far, I have presented a theological account of the assembly formed to participate in the ministry of the new evangelization through liturgical prayer. Such an assembly understands the various forms of liturgy as rites of return, occasions to be re-created by the triune God. Liturgical prayer capacitates this assembly to dwell in the space of gift, of love itself, to become an assembly of those being reformed into the image and likeness of God. The beauty of an assembly taken up into the logic of divine gift becomes a persuasive word to all those who encounter it.

Of course, what does it mean to say that something is beautiful? Beauty is by no means an uncontested term. Many of my students would say that beauty is "relative," dependent on the eye of the beholder. For some, a piece of art is considered kitschy, while for others it is the embodiment of loveliness. Music that pierces the eardrums of some provides an icon into human existence for others. In liturgy, the problem of beauty is often a contentious one. According to some, the beautiful liturgy consists of a proliferation of incense, of polyphonic music sung by a choir, of that encounter with the sacred and the transcendent God hidden in a mystery that invites us to silent adoration. On the other hand, as often articulated by my students, the attractive Eucharist is informal, places its emphasis not on expensive art and musical mastery but the beauty of the community, who joins together to sing music in hospitable places that warms the heart and unites voices into a gift of love.

There is another problem with discussing beauty in the context of a book on liturgy and the new evangelization. What allows us to assume that beauty is evangelizing in the first place? In other words, is it even important in the context of the new evangelization for a parish to consider the beauty of its liturgy, architecture, music, and liturgical celebration? Rather than ask what is beautiful, perhaps the pivotal question is to discern what is strategically effective, what draws an assembly together in the art of self-giving love, which is the *telos* of the liturgical life of the church to begin with.

This latter question must be dealt with before the former. That "beauty" has had a role in evangelization seems historically undeniable. Early Christians were initiated in baptisteries, bursting with biblical artwork and ritual that captured the imaginations of the initiate, bodily inscribing them into the gift of Christian faith.[10] Beauty in medieval Christianity elevated the human imagination through spiritual writings, the architecture of churches and music, and the eucharistic feast of Corpus Christi with the subsequent biblical drama and procession.[11] Our Lady of Guadalupe manifests herself to Juan Diego through flowers, song, and the beautiful image imprinted upon his cloak —thus incarnating the Gospel within the social imaginary of the native people.[12] The Oxford Movement in the nineteenth century employed the beauty of architectural flourish upon the altar in order to foster dispositions of eucharistic adoration, cultivating a piety previously absent.[13] Raïssa Maritain's Christ-centered poetry written in the midst of the Shoah formed the imaginations of Catholics and non-Catholics alike as she bestowed a voice of pained beauty to the suffering of millions of European Jews.[14] The Orthodox composer John Tavener has created a work of beauty in incarnating the narrative of the creation and fall of humanity and the resurrection of Jesus Christ, offering to the modern person a deeper awareness of the wonder of what it means to be human in Christ Jesus.[15]

Simply, it is impossible to deny that beauty, including that enshrined and learned within the liturgical rites of the church, has been integral to the evangelization of the Gospel within culture. Beauty, mediated through an encounter with bodily, ritual practice, a piece of visual or musical artwork, or the architectural design of a space:

> can move our heart at is depths, bringing us to a state in which we are open to seeing Christ and imagining the reign of God he came to usher in. Aesthetics is about hope and the "theological dimension of art lies in that, ultimately, art interprets humanity to the human." In this, art mirrors and makes transparent one of the ways Christ brings salva-

tion. Just as a poet sees the wonder that art evokes as "the reinvention of humility" and "the means by which we fall in love with the world," so the faith that Jesus preaches and lives is best embodied as "admitting human powerlessness," which then opens us "to something other, something new, something to come." [16]

Beauty invites each of us to participate in this process of returning to the Father, of imaging possibilities of a world transfigured in Christ. The beauty of the liturgical rites that we perform is not ancillary to the work of the new evangelization. It fosters within us a deeper capacity for love, for giving ourselves away to the triune God, who seeks to enter into relationship with us. Parishes that concern themselves with the beauty of liturgical practice are not wasting time, avoiding important strategic concerns related to intellectual and moral formation. The parish captivated by liturgical beauty seeks to offer a space in which the fullness of our perceptions, our desires, and everything that makes us human might be transfigured through the captivating beauty of a God who loves unto the end.

Of course, the question of what constitutes an evangelizing liturgical beauty remains unanswered. I would like to suggest four facets of a theological conception of a humanizing beauty, which should infuse liturgical worship. Liturgical beauty 1) begins with revelation, 2) is a gift received, 3) involves difference, 4) and is sacramental. As appropriate, I will draw attention to specific aspects of liturgical practice and space as essential to this notion of an evangelizing, liturgical beauty.

The Beauty of Revelation

For Christians, our notion of liturgical beauty is shaped first by allowing the form of God's beauty revealed through Jesus Christ to attune us to the wonder of divine beauty. At face value, there is nothing intrinsically beautiful to the crucifix in many of our churches. The human form is often stretched to its limits; the expression of pain on the face of Jesus may be tangible. Blood drips from the wounds of this man hung upon the tree. If I encountered a man or woman on the side of the road in a similar state, my first reaction would be to turn away my gaze in horror. Such an image of suffering might activate within me *pathos*, a deep sense of pity for the plight of my fellow mortal. But I would not say that the sight of this suffering was *beautiful.* Yet, millions of Christians contemplatively gaze upon this man stretched upon the tree discerning there an icon of the beauty of God's self-giving love.

The cross is central to forming our imagination relative to the radical notion of beauty operative in the Christian imaginative. Beauty is not merely that which pleases our senses. Christian beauty is known first and foremost through the form of revelation, of the decisive encounter of God with humanity in Jesus Christ now incarnate in the memory of the church. As Hans Urs von Balthasar writes regarding such a notion of beauty:

> just as we can never attain to the living God in any way except through his Son become man, but in this Son we can really attain to God in himself, so, too, we ought never to speak of God's beauty without reference to the form and manner of appearing which he exhibits in salvation-history. The beauty and glory which are proper to God may be inferred and "read" off from God's epiphany and its incomprehensible glory which is worthy of God himself.[17]

Thus, we come to know the depths of divine beauty through immersing ourselves into salvation history, into a contemplative encounter with the Word of God. A Christian notion of beauty is not an idea or an abstraction. It is a deeper immersion into the particularities of the mystery of divine love enshrined in salvation history: "In the end, that within Christianity, which draws persons to itself is a concrete and particular beauty, because a concrete and particular beauty *is its deepest truth*." [18]

Liturgical beauty must therefore begin with a contemplative gaze directed toward the history of salvation, seeking to manifest for the assembly this redemptive narrative through the liturgical life of the church. An example drawn from architecture might be of assistance here. Several years ago, I attended a newly built church in the Midwest. The space was full of natural light. The windows looked out upon manicured trees and bushes. The sanctuary of the church was carpeted and the walls were off-white. The only artwork on display was a disproportionally large statue of the Holy Family, a Celtic cross without the corpus, a tabernacle held by two hands, and a rather inconspicuous Stations of the Cross. The baptismal font was located outside the entrance into the sanctuary. When I asked one of the parishioners why there was a noticeable absence of imagery throughout the space, I was told that the pastor hoped that the beauty of natural light might infuse the church. After all, the beauty of creation is a gift from God, and thus it should be evident in our churches.

The architectural decision to exclude an array of Christian imagery is evidence of a neglect of the beauty of revelation in the design of the space. An idea, only peripherally drawn from the history of salvation, the role of natural light,[19] becomes the guiding ethos for the design of church. Indeed, it is possible that such a theological perspective could become a rather successful approach to designing a liturgical space. Churches need not be dark and stuffy places in order for salvation to take place. But the prevailing mood of the church was more akin to the suburban mall, the school auditorium, where we gather to enact our own therapeutic rites. Duncan Stroik writes:

> According to conventional wisdom, the best solution for a new church in suburbia is a building on a large piece of property elegantly hidden from view by trees and planting. Religion distances itself from all but the initiates. Like the private country club, it becomes a wonderful place to escape to be with other like-minded people. This "worship center" becomes a pleasant environment that people journey to once a week for their spiritual needs, not unlike a trip to the library or health space. The statement this type of building makes is that religion is good for your personal life and may help you become a better person.[20]

Such an approach to liturgical architecture ignores the drama of salvation, which takes place in every parish when it gathers to celebrate the rites of baptism, the anointing of the sick, the Sunday Eucharist, the Rite of Penance, and the Liturgy of the Hours.

Liturgical architecture and the imagery it employs within the space must become a dazzling manifestation of that divine revelation taking place in liturgical prayer; the engagement of our human senses in the process of salvation. A plurality of imagery in our churches invites us to remember the great deeds of salvation, to allow them to become implanted upon our bodies, our memories, and our desires.[21] Such imagery becomes a prophetic proclamation that God's own notion of beauty, of what constitutes an authentic human life, is interruptive of other societal narratives that are not saving. Further, the beauty of such imagery, its capacity to lift the mind and heart in wonder, allows us to participate in salvation itself. When my infant son attends the Basilica of the Sacred Heart at Notre Dame, although he is not able at this age to comprehend the homily or the Eucharistic Prayer, he can contemplate the incarnation of light through saints inscribed in stained glassed windows that evoke an aboriginal wonder within him. Through such preconscious wonder, he participates in the mystery of salvation in no less of a manner than the greatest academic theologian present in the same space. In treating, this contemplative, participatory quality to ecclesial architecture, Denis McNamara writes:

When there is a general consensus that a church doesn't "look like" one, the building has usually given up an attempt to make a distinct ecclesial architecture. Every church building is, to some degree, a record of the story of its people, but it should not simply be a projection of the earthly congregation. This would make it a decidedly unsacramental building, revealing only the visible realities of the fallen world. A properly designed church building reveals not only the people who built it, but the pilgrimage of the whole human race journeying toward the heavenly Jerusalem which is strengthened by drinking from the springs of divine life in the sacraments. The church therefore reveals also what the members of the congregation *hope to be* when fully nourished by divine life.[22]

Thus, liturgical beauty for the evangelization will recommit the church to inscribing our ecclesial spaces with imagery drawn from salvation history, pointing us toward our beatific destiny as creatures made in the image and likeness of God. Of course, this attention to biblical imagery, icons of saints, and the centrality of the cross in the life of the church is true also of liturgical music, of homilies, and of the catechetical ministry of the church. Such beauty is not a mere idea, a proposition. It is the drama of the narrative of salvation that is played out here and now through tangible signs.

The Gift of Beauty

For many, the created order simply passes before us as the background to our lives. We anxiously hurry upon city streets running to our next appointment unaware of the world around us. We jog past gorgeous valleys, flowered fields, listening to music to distract us from the physical exhaustion of such exercise. Rarely, in such a hurried state, do we allow creation to bestow itself as the gift it is; to see the world as it really is. During my doctoral studies I often walked back and forth to Boston College, meandering through the neighborhoods of Newton, Massachusetts. In the fall, the stunning foliage interspersed with gorgeous colonial homes, bestowed to me an image of what constitutes a New England town. It gave me a sense of what a city could be, a place in which human beings dwelled together in the natural order, cultivating a life of gift.

Beauty comes to us as this kind of gift, a poetic invitation to see reality as it is. Such beauty is not violence, a way of communicating ideology through attractive forms. The images of photoshopped models on the covers of magazines are not beautiful (even if they are sexy), because they exist outside of gift. They are a form of violence, which seeks to sell to us an image of what constitutes human flourishing connected to specific products; to raise our desires against our wills. It sells to us a desire to connect specific products with a form of Eros, of sexual attraction. The beauty of the crucifix is not that it seeks to cajole us into a certain affective state in which belief becomes possible. Its beauty comes through the invitation to perceive the cross for what it is—the self-offering of the God-Man that transforms the created order into a space of peace.

Thus, liturgical beauty, if it is to participate in this logic of gift at the heart of the narrative of salvation, will seek to raise our desires to the living God as a gift of love. Liturgical prayer operates as a kind of poetics, wooing us toward this God, suasively not violently. Poetics

> is that quality of language, verified to greater or lesser degree, which in its imaginative use includes reference to what is beyond immediate perception and everyday functional discourse. . . . Poetic language strains for what may come to light through innovative and imaginative expression. . . . It is always open to that fresh reading and hearing within which its power is newly revealed. Besides what is transmitted through texts and rites, there can also be a poetic turn of verbal or nonverbal character of a more passing quality in each celebration, by which the immediately present is lit up, but then passes from view. The way the sun shines through a window at a particular moment of a celebration, the way in which the newly lit candle flickers, the turn of a phrase used in a homily or a prayer, the way in which a parent answers the question of what is sought through baptism, belong to the poetic of actual liturgical celebrations.[23]

The question of beauty in liturgical worship is thus more than the concern of the aesthete. Seeking a certain poetics, a gifted and revelatory nature to human action and word, is required for liturgical celebration.

A beautiful, and thus poetic, liturgical celebration requires an economic use of speech upon the part of the presider relative to the rite. Too often presiders reduce the ritual aspects of liturgical prayer to ideas. Now we light this candle as a sign that Christ is the Light of the World. Such reductions eliminate the silent contemplation necessary for aesthetic insight. The beauty of liturgical prayer is actually experiencing, absent intellectual commentary, how Christ is the Light of the World, a light that shines even into the darkness of this community, of my own individual joys and suffering. It comes as a gift, as we recognize a truth implanted deeply within the human heart. The space in which we gather, the economy of words employed by the presider, and the silence of the space open us up to a renewed perception of the created order as a gift to be received.

Likewise, liturgical music can easily become, as in certain forms of praise and worship, emotional manipulation. Or, as in some contemporary music, there may be a communication of an ideology rather than doxology or lament. Relative to praise and worship, this emotional manipulation in liturgical music constantly risks a form of violence in which music does not lead to the reasonable offering of the assembly to the Father through the Son but a Dionysian intoxication that manipulates the human affections.[24] I have attended far too many young ministry gatherings in which the music of eucharistic adoration does not cultivate the offering of a wounded heart to the Father in love but a violent movement of the affections; what the teens would call "cry night." Indeed, the affections are intrinsic to Christian worship, since every facet of our humanity must be included. But when our affections are manipulated, when we are forced into a conversion, we no longer participate in a Eucharist of peace but a liturgy of our own passions.

Likewise, hymns—a perhaps unsuspected but felicitous development in the postconciliar Roman Rite—ought to be a form of theological poetry expanding the imagination of the assembly.[25] The poetics of such music is not that it invites me to contemplate myself, the holiness of my own particular identity as a Christian. Too often in parishes I have sung hymns that rejoiced in the enactment of divine justice in the present moment, as if such justice was reserved only for those outside of this liturgical assembly. Such speech is not doxological, directed toward praise, but self-praise. David Bentley Hart, commenting upon the manner in which human speech comes to be re-formed according to the gift of divine speech, writes:

> God's speech in creation does not, then, invite a speculative nisis toward silence—the silence of pure knowing or of absolute saying—but doxology, an overabundance of words, hymnody, prayer, and then, within this discipline of gratitude and liturgy, a speculative discourse obedient to the gratuity of existence and the transcendence of its source, or a contemplative silence whose secret is not poverty but plenitude.[26]

This principle of gift, of the peaceful offering of human desire in doxological wonder to the triune God, is exemplified in various hymn texts. Samuel J. Stone's hymn text, "The Church's One Foundation," is an embodiment of such an *ecumenical*, liturgical poetics, capacitating the liturgical participant to see the reality of ecclesial life as gift. Presently, I quote verses 1, 3, and 5:

The Church's one foundation
is Jesus Christ her Lord;
She is his new creation
By water and the word:
From heavn' he came and sought her
To be his holy bride;
With his own blood he bought her,
And for her life he died.

Though with a scornful wonder
Men see her sore opprest,
By schisms rent asunder,
By heresies distrest;
Yet saints their watch are keeping,
Their cry goes up, "How long?"
And soon the night of weeping
Shall be the morn of song.

Yet she on earth hath union
With God, the Three in One,
And mystic sweet communion
With those whose rest is won.
O happy ones and holy!
Lord, give us grace that we
Like them, the meek and lowly,
On high may dwell with thee.[27]

The images in the first verse immerse the singer into the salvific, sacramental nature of the church. The church is not a mere gathering of individuals, the assembly of those who have earned salvation through their own merits. The church consists of those baptized into the nuptial relationship of self-gift offered by the Son. Images are presented to the imagination, inviting one to a new understanding of what constitutes ecclesial identity. Likewise, in the third verse, the church's identity is poetically located between the lives of the saints and the reality of a humanity still being formed into the image and likeness of God. The church is in the process of salvation, and the entire communion of saints awaits the church's transformation into the fullness of doxology, of praise. The impoverished beauty of the church receives its final note in verse five, as even in the midst of such darkness, such schism, we celebrate in song the church's deepest reality as the body of believers who enjoy "mystic sweet communion" with the triune God. Liturgical hymnody should invite us to this degree of contemplation, an opportunity to perceive the gift of salvation, even in the midst of violence within the church, through the pedagogy of aesthetic delight.

Yet, the poetics of gift is not simply about the various liturgical arts available within the church's repertoire. The poesis of liturgical prayer brings us to the very gift of our lives, which we bring to the liturgical encounter. Human beings create poetry, they make art and music, and simultaneously they form poetic lives of gift to the world. William Dyrness writes:

> all the little projects, or stories, provide the material out of which we seek to construct a good life. The individual events are like so many notes, which we struggle to compose into a melody. Aristotle held that the fundamental impulse in the poetic imagination was "mimesis" or imitation. Dramatic action, what we are calling the figuration of our lives, may then be called creative imitation in the form of action. Imitation, which Aristotle says is, like desire, natural to us as humans, speaks of the charged character of the situation in which we live our lives . . . it also indicates the work of bricolage that makes up the figuring action of our lives, in which pieces and events are brought together into some aesthetic order.[28]

I have never understood why pastors, catechists, and liturgists seem so distraught that half-emptied churches are filled to the brim on Christmas and Easter. Those who attend liturgy these days are seeking some deeper meaning in their lives, some sense of divine relationship. Such moments of return, whether during key liturgical seasons or sacraments, are opportunities to invite parents and children alike to perceive the gift of salvation available in the church's rites, as well as to discern anew how these iconic moments of liturgical love might provide an aesthetic, holistic order to their lives. A couple, not active in the church, may slowly learn to see how the gift of their new child is in fact an occasion for eucharistic wonder. The feast of Easter is a moment in which the fullness of the hope of redemption can be an orienting gift to a life of a young adult, who is seeking some deeper meaning in life. Human beings look for meaning, for imagery, for narratives to understand our lives within the world. The liturgical life of the church provides such rich imagery and narrative, which allows human beings to live poetically and thus beautifully.

The Beauty of Difference

Christian notions of beauty emerge fundamentally from salvation history, opening us to the gift of the world around us, inviting us to perceive our very existence as an occasion for a liturgical poetics. Yet, equally important for beauty is difference. On my drive to school, in the midst of the lush fields and trees of northern Indiana, there is one enormous tree utterly devoid of life. It stretches out over the road, a menacing figure in the midst of the comfortable landscape of Midwestern life. The tree, otherwise unremarkable, becomes for the one attentive to its presence an encounter with beauty precisely as it stands out from the other trees. It is different.

Beauty involves difference. No one desires to listen to music with the same note repeated again and again. No one wants to attend an art gallery filled with copies of the same painting. The function of the French hymnody and Latin chant used throughout the film *Of Gods and Men* is to create a moment of difference in which the beauty of liturgical offering stands in stark contrast to the violence of the Algerian rebels. Commenting on the role of difference in beauty, Alejandro García-Rivera writes:

> God, who did not have to create any particular beings at all and who could have created a universe different from this one, created *this* one out of love for its own uniqueness. An omnipotent God who creates a particular, unique universe does so out of love for its own unique beauty. This answer reveals a God who loves difference, *this* difference. By loving the universe into being, God ordered the universe not according to the laws of design but by the laws of the "heart." In other words, the universe is ordered less by the laws of design than by the laws of the love of difference. The love of difference orders the world in ways that a machine would never be designed.[29]

Liturgical prayer becomes beautiful, and thus evangelical, when it embodies a love for difference. Such difference should be present in the way that the celebrant prays various parts of the Eucharistic Prayer, changing his voice depending upon the genre of the prayer text. It should be present within our celebration of the liturgical year; our ecclesial space should breathe the diverse signs of Lent, of Easter, of Ordinary Time. The commitment to aesthetically and theologically sound architecture is not a canonization of European Gothic and Romantic architecture alone. Churches in San Antonio, Texas, will embody distinctive imagery and style from ones in South Bend, Indiana. Catholicism throughout the globe provides ample imagery, devotional energy, and distinctive approaches to incarnating the Gospel that elevates the entirety of the sacramental and liturgical life of the church. Liturgical difference is not a problem to be solved, but an opportunity for the new evangelization. The success of World Youth Day within Catholicism is that it presents an image of a church of beautiful differences united in sharing the self-giving love of the God-Man, Jesus Christ.

Of course, the recognition of difference is not always easy. Parish life, ideally, should be one of difference. Parishes include the poor and the rich; those active within the ministries of the parish and those with limited financial and social commitment; those recently born and those who are approaching death. Such difference is evidence of how every facet of our humanity is to be transformed in Christ. The humanity of the new couple, struggling to keep their newborn silent during Mass, is part of the beautiful difference. The homeless woman, wandering in and out of the church during the Eucharist, is part of the beautiful difference. The elderly gentleman, who attends early Sunday morning Mass hoping to never speak to another person in the parish, is part of the beautiful difference. The adolescent, undergoing the first doubts in his life of faith, is part of the beautiful difference. The young man recently arrived from the Philippines, struggling to adjust to American culture, is part of the beautiful difference. It is the very particularity of our humanity that the liturgy takes up, transforming beautiful difference into liturgical gift.

The beauty of difference is what enables our liturgy to be human, and thus a moment of evangelization. We do not need to "create" liturgical events that come off perfectly. We do not need to force every person in the parish to perform gestures in the precise same manner. I encountered liturgists who argue that no one should be denied communion for their politics, but then in the very next breath state that they would like to curb excessive bowing and adoration of the Eucharist in their parishes. Liturgical formation, which seeks to erase difference, becomes an act of violence to the person. The true beauty of the liturgical life is that all of our differences, all of our various practices, are taken up into the liturgical prayer of the church and become essential to our re-formation into the image and likeness of God.

The Sacramentality of Beauty

I remember the first time that I looked into the eyes of my son (who graced me with five minutes of wakefulness on day two of his life), suddenly aware of a capacity for a love that I had never imagined possible. Of course, the beauty of the moment was not simply his eyes, which were barely open. It was the beauty of recognizing for one moment that this human being was putting the entirety of his trust in me. It was the intimate exchange of a love not yet capable of words, yet shared in the silent discourse of a father feeding his child in the early morning. Such beauty was not merely physical; it was a spiritual communion of one person with another. The beauty of the moment, the exquisite gift of gazing into his eyes, gave way to the more mundane aspects of parenthood including changing diapers, getting up in the middle of night for a feeding, and arranging babysitting for nights away from home. But the spiritual reality of love remained.

Indeed, the liturgical life of the church bestows to us a glimpse into divine beauty, an image of self-giving love, which culminates in the offering of ourselves in amorous silence. Yet such beauty inevitably fades away. If one simply looks at the architecture of the church, then quite literally the physical plant slowly falls apart as time takes its toll. Hymnody that once captured our imaginations with its beauty becomes mundane, perhaps boring. We pray at Lauds with voices too exhausted, too tired, to attend with any degree of attention to the sheer beauty of the psalms.

The beauty of the church's liturgy does not operate simply at face value. Beauty is sacramental, a sign that points us toward some spiritual reality, which is even more beautiful because it is divine. Certainly, one would not want to discount the value of the sign, the importance of beautiful artwork, of musical texts, of the physicality of our bodies. But, we have all encountered elderly couples whose physical beauty has slowly faded away with the advance of age. The manner in which this couple holds hands, attends to each other's deepest needs, points us toward the spiritual reality of the permanence of love. When memory itself begins to fade from one of the spouses (as it too often does), still beauty remains as the other spouse embodies love through patiently attending to the gradual decline of the beloved.

The sacramentality of beauty is essential to liturgical prayer in particular. Not every liturgical action or space embodies the aesthetics described above. Lectors fumble over words, distorting the narrative of salvation. The collect prayers in the Missal might at times be awkward, leading to puzzlement rather than contemplative delight. The psalmody ascribed for morning and evening prayer may become boring in our third and fourth years of praying the Office. Our fellow member of the assembly, whose particular gift is not music, may very well deform the sacrifice of praise into a cry for help. The moral life of the priest, who acts in the person of Christ and the church in our liturgical celebrations, might not be a rich icon of sanctity but an impoverished portrait of darkness and degradation. Even the most "aesthetically" pleasing liturgical rite may call to mind not the beauty of Christ's self-gift but a church (in both lay and clerical leadership) that too often seeks power and prestige above the poverty of self-gift. In the midst of such squalor, in the midst of such darkness, the beauty of divine life continues to become incarnate.

This sacramental nature of beauty is not something that we come to recognize spontaneously. It requires attunement to self-emptying love. Hans Urs von Balthasar describes this process of attuning our affections to the measure of Christ's self-gift:

> What is here involved is not only an objectless and intentionless dis-position (*Stimmung*), but rather a deliberate attunement of self (*sich-Einstimmen*) to the accord (*Stimmen*) existing between Christ and his mandate from the Father, in the context of salvation-history's assent (*Zu-stimmung*), which the Holy Spirit *is* in Christ and effects in him. We speak, therefore, primarily of an empathy (*Mitfühlen*) with the Son who renounces the form of God and chooses the form of humiliation; we speak of a sense for the path taken by Christ which leads him to the Cross.[30]

We come to see the sacramental beauty of the church's liturgical rites even in the midst of ugliness insofar as we give ourselves over to the kenotic love of the Son. Indeed, the music sung at the eucharistic liturgy may be both out of tune and inappropriate for the season at hand. The homilist may offer a less than stunning account of salvation history. Still, human beings seek to raise their voices to God, to give ourselves over to the Father through the Son in the unity of the Holy Spirit through the poverty of human praise.

The deeper sacramental nature of beauty is in fact deeply evangelizing. Of course, we must attend to the signs of our liturgical celebrations, seeking a liturgy that reveals the gift of a God who loves unto the end. But, we must remind ourselves, as John Henry Newman preached:

> A thick black veil is spread between this world and the next. We mortal men range up and down it, to and fro, and see nothing. There is no access through it into the next world. In the Gospel this veil is not removed; it remains, but every now and then marvelous disclosures are made to us of what is behind it. At times we seem to catch a glimpse of a Form which we shall hereafter see face to face. We approach, and in spite of the darkness, our hands, or our head, or our brow, or our lips become, as it were, sensible of the contact of something more than earthly. We know not where we are, but we have been bathing in water, and a voice tells us that it is blood. Or we have a mark signed upon our foreheads, and it spake of Calvary. Or we recollect a hand laid upon our heads, and surely it had the print of nails in it, and resembled His who with a touch gave sight to the blind and raised the dead. Or we have been eating and drinking; and it was not a dream surely, that One fed us from His wounded side, and renewed our nature by the heavenly meat He gave.[31]

In the end, the rites of the church are beautiful not because of our own capacity for aesthetic design, for spending lavishly upon incense and chalices, because our music imitates the transcendent beauty of the cosmos itself. Instead, the sacramental beauty of liturgical prayer is that Christ comes to us through the rites that we participate in. To give ourselves over to this way of life, with firm reliance that God will pierce through the veil of this darkness with the light of his love, is to assume a posture of evangelical wonder within the cosmos. To pray liturgically is to perform a sacramental beauty proper to the vocation of the one being re-created into the image and likeness of God.

A Lay Movement for the Liturgical New Evangelization

This chapter has focused on how every liturgical action of the church is a rite of return, an invitation for humanity to become as beautiful as the God who gives himself in the foolishness of crucified love. Yet, many of those who most need to hear this narrative are not lining up at the doors of our parishes awaiting the opportunity to engage in the liturgical and sacramental life of the church. They are not watching with eager anticipation the television advertisements inviting them to come home to the life of the church. They are some of the students in my classroom, who are seeking for meaning in life but find it difficult to submit to the dictates of a church that allowed a sexual abuse crisis. Their spiritual lives are devoid of specific content or an institutional form except that of being decent human beings. Yet, the degree to which these emerging adults are lost, wandering without a deeper meaning in life, is far too real. Turning to Christian Smith's recent analysis of the state of these emerging adults:

> We are failing to teach them how to deal constructively with moral, cultural, and ideological differences. We are failing to teach them to think about what is good for people and in life. We are failing to equip our youth with the ideas, tools, and practices to know how to negotiate their romantic and sexual lives in healthy, nondestructive ways that prepare them to achieve the happy, functional marriages and families that most of them say they want in future years. We are failing to teach our youth about life purposes and goals that matter more than the accumulation of material possessions and material comfort and security. We are failing to challenge the too common need to be intoxicated, the apparent inability to live a good, fun life without being under the influence of alcohol or drugs. And we are failing to teach our youth the importance of civic engagement and political participation, how to be active citizens of their communities and nations, how to think

about and live for the common good . . . we in the older adult world
are failing youth and emerging adults in these crucial ways *because our
own adults world is itself also failing* in those same ways.[32]

The church's mission of the new evangelization, of incarnating the Gospel
into every sphere of social life, of fostering a renewed commitment of those
now lapsed Catholics through the revitalization of a theological and sacramental imagination transformative of human experience, must respond to
this present state of adult life.

Yet, the very nature of our parishes is often designed for the committed, those already in the liturgical and sacramental life of the church. But
as the Gospel makes clear, the triune God is not simply interested in taking
care of those who are already present. We profess faith in a God who combs
the highways and the byways for the ragged who want to attend the great
banquet of generosity; a God who foolishly searches for a single sheep; a
God who turns a house upside down to find one coin; a God who endures
the pain of ingratitude from younger and older son alike, yet rejoices when
they return (cf. Luke 14:15-24; 15:1-32). Baptized into the prodigal logic of
such a God, our only option is to imitate such self-emptying love. To become
what we received, a gift for the life of the world.

If the new evangelization is to have its full effect, then it will become necessary for the entire parish to cease maintaining the *status quo*. Parishes will
become centers for evangelization, moving outside the walls of the building
into the city, the suburb, the rural landscape. For a moment, allow me to perform a thought experiment based in my present hometown of South Bend,
Indiana. South Bend is a small city with a population of little over 100,000
permanent residents (in addition to a number of undocumented immigrants).
Within the city are a variety of institutions of higher learning. The parishes
are well established with both active schools and committed parishioners.
Yet, there are many young adults in the area seeking something more, who
find themselves entrapped in cultures that promote massive consumptions
of alcohol and sexual promiscuity. At Notre Dame, they summarize such an
attitude as "work hard and play hard." Likewise in downtown South Bend,
one encounters any number of homeless men and women suffering from the
plight of poverty, of loneliness, and of drug addiction. South Bend, despite
its rather substantive Catholic identity vis-à-vis cities such as Boston and
New York, is a ripe field for mission.

Suppose then that a group of lay people from various parishes in the
area purchased a site downtown, affiliated with the local parishes, but dedi-

cated solely to a form of outreach based in liturgical prayer. These lay people, themselves committed to the prodigal love embodied in the liturgical and sacramental life of the church but whose vocations are especially connected to the cultivation of the world, would practice the beauty of Catholic faith within the city. Lay preaching would take place every evening in the context of the Liturgy of the Hours and all-night Vigils, as well as in other paraliturgical and devotional prayer, including candlelit Taizé, the rosary, and eucharistic adoration. A space would be available to those wandering the bars of downtown to come in and pray, to talk with someone in the middle of the night. Lectures, talks, and sermons on topics relevant to living the Christian life would be given over the course of the year, based not in suburban parishes but in the heart of the city. The entire diocese would be invited to attend these events; downtown would become a place for all parishes to gather, to embody the eucharistic love at the heart of Catholic existence. The poor, the hungry, the suffering would be given a meal, job training, whatever was needed to help them live lives of human flourishing, of the sort of self-gift embodied in the eucharistic life of the church.

In many ways, such communities already exist. What would set this group apart is the centrality of persuasive preaching and of living the liturgical and sacramental life in the context of the city. Sunday Eucharist would still occur in the context of parish life; this community would be sustained by the liturgical preaching of the deacon, the priest, and the bishop. But the specific charism of such a community, dedicated to the work of the new evangelization, would be liturgical: to become a living sign of the way in which our humanity comes to be transformed by the liturgical prayer of the church. Those who struggle, who suffer, who desire something more, should have a space in which the living God comes to heal woundedness and transform it into a gift of total love.

Indeed, such a community will struggle. It will be difficult to be so public in this proclamation of faith. Each member of this community would need spiritual direction, submitting oneself to a process of learning to embody liturgical gift. Pastoral training would be required, allowing these lay people to serve as friends to those suffering from the wounds of a world too often deaf to the deepest desires of the human heart for love. But such a community, dedicating itself to the transformation of the world through liturgical prayer, through communal life, through preaching the Word of God, might slowly transform hearts to perceive how every aspect of culture and every part of human desire can be lifted up to the Father in love. The Christian life is not simply a catalogue of rules and regulations, which are intended to deny our humanity. Instead, such a community would be a sacramental sign of the joy, of the aesthetics of the kingdom, offering the gift of a life to the Father through the Son in the unity of the Holy Spirit.

———————————————

Liturgical prayer is essential to the new evangelization. Precisely, because in every liturgical rite, we human beings return to our vocation as those made in the image and likeness of God. We are capacitated for the kind of self-gift, which comes to transfigure society. Those who return to our sacramental life should encounter there a beautiful and humanizing liturgy, one that elevates the desires of the human heart, allowing them to become an offering of love to the Father. We are immersed in a cosmos in which the primary narrative is not one of grasping, seizing, but the prodigal logic of self-gift. Lay communities, connected to parishes, may incarnate this liturgical life in concrete ways in cities and rural areas as we seek to manifest to the world that wisdom of a Catholic life, given over to the sacramental logic of the triune God.

This final chapter is a fitting conclusion to a work on liturgy and the new evangelization. Again, the new evangelization does not seek to cajole, to convince through an act of rhetorical or intellectual violence that one must become a better Catholic. Instead, the new evangelization is a spiritual renewal of the entire life of the parish, an opening of our eyes and hearts to the reality that we are made for the art of self-giving love. The liturgical life of the church, embodied in preaching, in our structure of praying, in our desire for sacramental beauty, is a pedagogy into this art form of self-gift. As our parishes learn to assume this vocation of self-gift, to operate according to a love that we have first received, then others will be attracted by this way of life. And for a moment, like John in the book of Revelation, we will begin to a see a glimpse of our beatific destiny:

> Then I saw a new heaven and a new earth; for the first heaven and the first earth had passed away, and the sea was no more. And I saw the holy city, the new Jerusalem, coming down out of heaven from God, prepared as a bride adorned for her husband. And I heard a loud voice from the throne saying, "See the home of God is among mortals. He will dwell with them; they will be his peoples, and God himself will be with them, and he will wipe every tear from their eyes. Death will be no more; mourning and crying and pain will be no more, for the first things have passed away." And the one who was seated on the throne said, "See, I am making all things new." (Rev 21:1-5)

In the liturgical life of the heavenly city our humanity does not disappear. Our tears, our wounds, are wiped away by the abiding presence of a God, who dwells with the people. Even now, in the midst of our mourning over the dead, of our rejoicing at married life, of the regular celebration of the Eucharist, the triune God comes to dwell among us and give us a glimpse, through the humanity of our liturgical rites, of what God has imagined for the human race. *Lift up your hearts. We lift them up to the Lord.*

Afterword

As the final touches were being put on this book, Pope Francis released the post-synodal apostolic exhortation on the new evangelization, entitled *Evangelii Gaudium*. The promulgation of this document, *The Joy of the Gospel*, is thus by far the most comprehensive treatment of what constitutes the new evangelization by the magisterium. The style of the document, written in a personal tone that has come to characterize the papacy of Pope Francis, is intended not merely to communicate information to the universal church but to change the hearts of each person who undertakes a meditation upon its theme. As Pope Francis writes, "We become fully human when we become more than human, when we let God bring us beyond ourselves in order to attain the fullest truth of our being. Here we find the source and inspiration of all our efforts as evangelization. For if we have received the love which restores meaning to our lives, how can we fail to share that love with others?" (EG 8). Evangelization is not a denial of our humanity but is instead the fruit of a communal life given over to ruminating upon the merciful love of the Father revealed in the Son, now made present through the indwelling of the Spirit. The "novelty" of the new evangelization is in fact something old: "Whenever we make the effort to return to the source and to recover the original freshness of the Gospel, new avenues arise, new paths of creativity open up, with different forms of expression, more eloquent signs and words with new meaning for today's world. Every form of authentic evangelization is always 'new'" (EG 11).

I have hoped in this book to communicate via the liturgical task of the new evangelization a posture of eucharistic gratitude similar to that which is ubiquitous in *Evangelii Gaudium*. Indeed, it was heartening as a theologian concerned with the pastoral life of the church to see so many themes from my own book reflected in the apostolic exhortation. The centrality of Christ's own beauty in the life of the church, the need for a renewal in preaching, the significance of the Christian vocation to sanctify and transform the world through self-giving love—all of these themes (and more) receive pride of place in Pope Francis's articulation of the new evangelization.

Yet, in the limited space of an afterword (serving as a formal conclusion to this book), I wanted to draw the attention of the reader to Pope Francis's comments on liturgy and evangelization in particular: "Evangelization with joy becomes beauty in the liturgy, as part of our daily concern to spread goodness. The Church evangelizes and is herself evangelized through the beauty of the liturgy, which is both a celebration of the task of evangelization and the source of her renewed self-giving" (EG 24). The liturgical prayer of the Church is not then a distraction from the real work of transforming the world, of serving the poor, of reaching out to those on the margins. Rather, participation in liturgical prayer, especially in the Eucharist, inscribes the Christian life in the self-giving love of a God who dwells in these margins. Participation in this sacramental life is not reserved for those elite Christians who have ascended toward holiness: "The Eucharist, although it is the fullness of the sacramental life, is not a prize for the perfect but a powerful medicine and nourishment for the weak" (EG 47).

Pope Francis, in fact, holds two poles together that many in the church desperately seek to separate: beauty and justice. The beauty of the liturgy—however one conceives it—is not an idol meant to be adored. Throughout the document, Francis cautions readers against such idolatry: "In some people we see an ostentatious preoccupation for the liturgy, for doctrine and for the Church's prestige, but without any concern that the Gospel have a real impact on God's faithful people and the concrete needs of the present time" (EG 95). Here Pope Francis does not deny that beauty is pivotal to the new evangelization. Instead, those responsible for the liturgical life of the church need to acknowledge that the final end of the liturgical life is not the celebration of more liturgies. It is an encounter with the God who is beauty incarnate, a meeting that changes the very meaning of human life: "The Son of God, by becoming flesh, summoned us to the revolution of tenderness" (EG 88).

Thus the constant talk of liturgical reform—whether raised by self-denominating traditionalists or progressives—has become an obstacle to the new evangelization. These liturgical wars have deformed such prayer into an expression of our own idols, of what the experts want the church to become: "It always pains me greatly to discover how some Christian communities, and even consecrated persons, can tolerate different forms of enmity, division, calumny, defamation, vendetta, jealousy and the desire to impose certain ideas at all costs, even to persecutions which appear as veritable witch hunts" (EG 100). In reality, there are many forms of beauty manifested in the liturgical life of the church: "Every expression of true beauty can thus be acknowledged as a path leading to an encounter with the Lord Jesus" (EG 167). We must measure the beauty of our liturgical celebrations not simply according to the number of people involved in the rite, the quantity of incense used in the celebration, our understanding of how this rite conforms to what we thought the Second Vatican Council hoped to enact, or the choice of traditional or contemporary music. Liturgical prayer is not simply the personal expression of what a certain in-group finds beautiful, the idol of the pretty. Instead, we must constantly discern if our prayer points toward the beauty of Christ's self-gift to the Father, a beauty that is not self-referential but oriented toward the other: "Beyond all our own preferences and interests, our knowledge and motivations, we evangelize for the greater glory of the Father who loves us" (EG 267).

Yet, as Pope Francis makes clear, the beauty of the liturgy is not complete until it culminates in the liturgy of life. Pope Francis' apostolic exhortation is careful to attend to the social ills that plague the modern, human condition:

> How can it be that it is not a news item when an elderly homeless person dies of exposure, but it is news when the stock market loses two points? This is a case of exclusion. Can we continue to stand by when food is thrown away while people are starving? This is a case of inequality. Today everything comes under the laws of competition and the survival of the fittest, where the powerful feed upon the powerless. As a consequence, masses of people find themselves excluded and marginalized: without work, without possibilities, without any means of escape. (EG 53)

For those who read this apostolic exhortation outside of the Catholic imagination, Francis's social critique is a matter of partisan politics in which the new pontiff declares his allegiance to a specific political agenda. In fact, Pope Francis's emphasis on becoming a church of the poor, the powerless, one that reaches out to the margins of society, is an extension of his eucharistic and evangelical vision. Solidarity is for Pope Francis a eucharistic disposition that "presumes the creation of a new mindset which thinks in terms of community and the priority of the life of all over the appropriation of goods by a few" (EG 188). Yet such solidarity is not concerned with mere thought alone, a gathering of the gnostic elite who debate about a way to proceed in political and economic matters. Such solidarity requires that the Christian enter into the fullness of history, into the changing of social structures, and the renewal of one's own heart toward a deeper love of the poor who are "sacraments" of Christ's presence here and now. In this way, the new evangelization becomes the church's contribution to the entire human family: "I am firmly convinced that openness to the transcendent can bring about a new political and economic mindset which would help to break down the wall of separation between the economy and the common good of society" (EG 205).

Pope Francis's discourse around the social nature of evangelization is sacramental in structure. He cautions against becoming a church community that not only ignores the poor but soothes oneself by drifting "into a spiritual worldliness camouflaged by religious practices, unproductive meetings and empty talk" (EG 207). It is inadequate for any one specific church to embrace disembodied ideas: "Not to put the word into practice, not to make it reality, is to build on sand, to remain in the realm of pure ideas and to end up in a lifeless and unfruitful self-centeredness and gnosticism" (EG 233).

Thus, for Pope Francis, the liturgy is a celebration of the task of evangelization precisely because the memory of Christ's life, death, and resurrection is passed on in each culture that makes up the human family. The fullness of what constitutes human life is presented anew as the pilgrim church encounters the love of Christ made flesh in feasts and seasons. At the same time, it is the source of such self-giving love insofar as the reality proclaimed in the liturgical life of the Church must become flesh in time and space. Liturgical prayer can never become a self-enclosed universe where we champion our ideas, we savor our own poetry, or we delight in beauty for beauty's sake. As Benedict XVI himself wrote:

> Faith, worship, and *ethos* are interwoven as a single reality which takes shape in our encounter with God's *agape*. Here the usual contraposition between worship and ethics simply falls apart. "Worship" itself, Eucharistic communion, includes the reality both of being loved and of loving others in turn. A Eucharist which does not pass over into the concrete practice of love is intrinsically fragmented. Conversely . . . the "commandment" of love is only possible because it is more than a requirement. Love can be "commanded" because it has first been given. (*Deus Caritas Est* 14)

The liturgy is essential to the task of the new evangelization precisely because it empowers the Christian to perceive anew that the heart of existence is not an economy of scarcity founded upon a pragmatic individualism. It is love made flesh. All of life, even before we can first take a breath, is a gift received. We are made for eucharistic love. Exploring the implications of this reality, one proclaimed so freshly by Pope Francis, is the work not simply of theologians or catechists. This work is the responsibility of each Catholic sent forth from eucharistic worship, emboldened by the Spirit to proclaim through the gift of their entire selves the reality that God is love. The new evangelization is nothing less than the art of self-giving love.

Notes

Introduction—pages 1–7

1. Hans Urs von Balthasar, *Love Alone Is Credible*, trans. D. C. Schindler (San Francisco: Ignatius Press, 2004), 51–60.

2. New Testament references will be taken from the NRSV. Old Testament references from the Jewish Publication Society, Tanakh Translation.

3. *Lineamenta* 5, XIII Ordinary General Assembly, "The New Evangelization for the Transmission of the Christian Faith," accessed June 12, 2013, http://www.vatican.va/roman_curia/synod/documents/ rc_synod_doc_20110202_lineamenta-xiii-assembly_en.html.

4. Yet, even within this rite itself, there are several theological models operative that complicate any act of meaning making through the sacrament. See Mark Searle, "Infant Baptism Reconsidered," *Living Water, Sealing Spirit: Readings on Christian Initiation*, ed. Maxwell Johnson (Collegeville, MN: Liturgical Press, 1995), 365–410.

5. Rite of Baptism for Children, in *The Rites of the Catholic Church*, vol. 1 (Collegeville, MN: Liturgical Press, 1990), no. 9.

6. Ibid., no. 56.

7. Jean Corbon, *The Wellspring of Worship*, trans. Matthew J. O'Connell (San Francisco: Ignatius Press, 2005), 199.

Chapter 1—pages 9–34

1. Paul VI, *Evangelium Nuntiandi,* in *The Catechetical Documents: A Parish Resource,* ed. Martin Connell (Chicago: Liturgy Training Publications, 1996), no. 2.

2. Henri de Lubac, *Catholicism: Christ and the Common Destiny of Man*, trans. Lancelot C. Sheppard and Elizabeth Englund (San Francisco: Ignatius Press, 1988), 53.

3. *Lumen Gentium*, in *Vatican Council II: Constitutions, Decrees, Declarations*, ed. Austin Flannery (Northport, NY: Costello Publishing, 1996), no. 12. All quotations from the documents of Vatican II will be taken from this edition.

4. Joseph Ratzinger, *God Is Near Us: The Eucharist, the Heart of Life*, ed. Stephan Otto and Vinzenze Pfnür, trans. Henry Taylor (San Francisco: Ignatius Press, 2003), 114–15.

5. John Paul II, *Catechesi Tradendae* (Washington DC: USCCB Publishing, 1979), no. 18.

6. John Paul II, *Redemptor Hominis* (New York: Pauline Books, 2009), no. 10.

7. Jean Mouroux, *The Christian Experience: An Introduction to Theology*, trans. George Lamb (New York: Sheed and Ward, 1954), 189.

8. Nathan Mitchell, *Meeting Mystery: Liturgy, Worship, and Sacraments* (Maryknoll, NY: Orbis, 2006), 185–87; Louis-Marie Chauvet, *Symbol and Sacrament: A Sacramental Reinterpretation of Christian Existence*, trans. Patrick Madigan and Madeleine Beaumont (Collegeville, MN: Liturgical Press, 1995), 152–55.

9. *General Catechetical Directory,* in *The Catechetical Documents: A Parish Resource*, no. 18.

10. *General Directory for Catechesis* (Washington, DC: USCCB, 1997), 38.

11. Pope Francis, *General Audience*, April 17, 2013, accessed May 27, 2013, http://www.vatican.va/holy_father/ francesco/audiences/2013/documents /papa-francesco_20130417_udienza-generale_en.html.

12. Josef Jungmann, "Constitution on the Sacred Liturgy," trans. Lalit Adolphus, in *Commentaries on the Documents of Vatican II*, ed. Herbert Vorgrimler, vol. 1 (New York: Herder and Herder, 1967), 15.

13. Ibid., 9.

14. See Louis Bouyer, *The Liturgy Revived: A Doctrinal Commentary of the Conciliar Constitution on the Liturgy* (Notre Dame, IN: University of Notre Dame Press, 1964), 5–8.

15. Cyprian Vagaggini, *Theological Dimensions of the Liturgy: A General Treatise of the Liturgy*, 4th ed., trans. Leonard J. Doyle and W. A. Jurgens (Collegeville, MN: Liturgical Press, 1976), 3.

16. Yves Congar, *The Meaning of Tradition*, trans. A. N. Woodrow (San Francisco: Ignatius Press, 2004), 135.

17. Bruce Morrill, *Encountering Christ in the Eucharist: The Paschal Mystery in People, Word, and Sacrament* (New York: Paulist Press, 2012), 3–5.

18. Jungmann, "Constitution on the Sacred Liturgy," 11–12.

19. Odo Casel, *The Mystery of Christian Worship,* ed. Burkhard Neunheuser (New York: Crossroad, 1962).

20. Ibid., 3.

21. Ibid., 9.

22. Ibid.

23. Ibid., 13.

24. Ibid., 15.

25. Vagaggini, *Theological Dimensions of the Liturgy*, 15.

26. Benedict XVI, *Sacramentum Caritatis* (Boston: Pauline, 2007), no. 71.

27. Massimo Faggioli, *True Reform: Liturgy and Ecclesiology in Sacrosanctum Concilium* (Collegeville, MN: Liturgical Press, 2012), 15–18.

28. See Yves Congar, "The *Ecclesia* or Christian Community as a Whole Celebrates the Liturgy," in *At the Heart of Christian Worship: Liturgical Essays of Yves Congar*, trans. and ed. Paul Philibert (Collegeville, MN: Liturgical Press, 2010), 15–67.

29. Jungmann, "Constitution on the Sacred Liturgy," 15.

30. Louis Bouyer, *The Church of God: Body of Christ and Temple of the Holy Spirit*, trans. Charles Underhill Quinn (San Francisco: Ignatius Press, 2011), 281.

31. Joseph Cardinal Ratzinger, *Pilgrim Fellowship of Faith: The Church as Communion*, ed. Stephan Otto Horn and Vinzenz Pfnür, trans. Henry Taylor (San Francisco: Ignatius Press, 2005), 89.

32. J.-M.-R. Tillard, *Flesh of the Church, Flesh of Christ: At the Source of the Ecclesiology of Communion*, trans. Madeleine Beaumont (Collegeville, MN: Liturgical Press, 2001), 61.

33. Vagaggini, *Theological Dimensions of the Liturgy*, 39.

34. Ibid., 43.

35. Ibid., 47–61.

36. Ibid., 72–74.

37. Ibid., 74.

38. Ibid.

39. Ibid.

40. Ibid., 74.

41. Ibid., 125.

42. Geoffrey Wainwright, *Doxology: The Praise of God in Worship, Doctrine, and Life* (New York: Oxford University Press, 1980), 15–44.

43. Bouyer, *The Liturgy Revived*, 45.

44. Joseph Ratzinger, *The Spirit of the Liturgy*, trans. John Saward (San Francisco: Ignatius, 2000), 175.

45. Pamela Jackson, *An Abundance of Graces: Reflections on* Sacrosanctum Concilium (Chicago: Hillenbrand Books, 2004), 31–32.

Chapter 2—pages 35–50

1. John Paul II, *Redemptoris Missio* (Boston: Pauline, 1990), no. 33.

2. Claudio M. Burgaleta, "Benedict XVI and the New Evangelization," *Church Life: A Journal for the New Evangelization* 2 (2013): 55–60.

3. Benedict XVI, *Verbum Domini* (Boston: Pauline Books, 2010), no. 96.

4. United States Council of Catholic Bishops (USCCB), *National Directory for Catechesis* (Washington DC: USCCB, 2005), no. 29G.

5. Benedict XVI, *Caritas in Veritate*, in *Catholic Social Thought: A Documentary Heritage*, ed. David J. O'Brien and Thomas A. Shannon (Maryknoll, NY: Orbis Books, 2010), no. 56. See also, Jürgen Habermas and Joseph Ratzinger, *The Dialectics of Secularization: On Reason and Religion* (San Francisco: Ignatius Press, 2006).

6. See Charles Taylor's *A Secular Age* (Cambridge, MA: Belknap Press, 2009).

7. Charles Taylor, "A Catholic Modernity?" in *Dilemmas and Connections: Selected Essays* (Cambridge, MA: Belknap Press, 2011), 167–87.

8. Charles Taylor, *A Secular Age*, 3.

9. Ibid.

10. Christian Smith, *What Is a Person?: Rethinking Humanity, Social Life, and the Moral Good from the Person Up* (Chicago: University of Chicago Press, 2010), 301–2.

11. Smith cautions against this sociological fallacy of reductionism, implicitly presumed by a strong social constructionism: "Human beings . . . are free, ensouled creatures of a particular kind, with the kind of nature about which we must get over our mental and emotional difficulties admitting if we hope possibly to understand ourselves. Yet humans are also material, embodied animals, nurtured and sustained in a physical world governed by causal powers and laws and their natural effects that we cannot simply deconstruct away. When it comes to the human, therefore, reductionist moves either toward the physical or the mental, the material or the ideal, the corporeal or the spiritual are unacceptable and self-defeating. Humans are embodied souls who can only be understood and explained in light of that complex reality" (*What Is a Person?*, 22).

12. Christian Smith, "Introduction," in *The Secular Revolution: Power, Interests, and Conflict in the Secularization of American Public Life*, ed. Christian Smith (Berkeley, CA: University of California Press, 2003), 1–96.

13. In particular, see José Casanova, *Public Religions in the Modern World* (Chicago: University of Chicago Press, 1994); Grace Davie, *Europe—The Exceptional Case: Parameters of Faith in the Modern World* (London: Darton, Longman & Todd, 2002); David Martin, *On Secularization: Towards a Revised General Theory* (Burlington, VT: Ashgate, 2005), 123–40.

14. Christian Smith with Melinda Lundquist Denton, *Soul Searching: The Religious and Spiritual Lives of American Teenagers* (New York: Oxford University Press, 2005), 7.

15. For a lengthier account of the survey's methodology, see Christian Smith with Patricia Snell, *Souls in Transition: The Religious and Spiritual Lives of Emerging Adults* (New York: Oxford University Press, 2009), 319.

16. Emerging adults are, according to Smith and Snell, a stage of development between adolescence and adulthood, marked by "intense identity exploration, instability, a focus on self, feeling in limbo or in transition or in between, and a sense of possibilities, opportunities, and unparalleled hope" (*Souls in Transition*, 6).

17. For the results of the General Social Survey from 2010 to the present, see http://www.norc.org/ GSS+Website/ (accessed June 7, 2011).

18. Smith and Snell, *Souls in Transition*, 102.

19. Smith and Denton, *Soul Searching*, 34.

20. Ibid., 36–37.

21. Ibid., 111.

22. Smith, *What Is a Person?*, 184.

23. Smith and Snell, *Souls in Transition*, 4.

24. Smith and Denton, *Soul Searching*, 31.

25. Ibid., 86.

26. Smith and Snell, *Souls in Transition*, 106.

27. Ibid.,119.

28. Ibid., 141.

29. Ibid., 145–51.

30. Ibid., 206.

31. Smith and Snell, *Souls in Transition,* 146.

32. Robert Bellah, et al., *Habits of the Heart: Individualism and Commitment in American Life*, 3rd ed. (Berkeley, CA: University of California Press, 2008), 221.

33. Spiritual seeking is characterized by a concern to establish a personal basis for religious belief, cultivating a mystical sense of God's presence within the world, a distrust of institutional religion, and affirmation of the infinite potential of human development. See Robert C. Fuller, *Spiritual but not Religious: Understanding Unchurched America* (New York: Oxford University Press, 2001), 75–77.

34. Believing without belonging is maintaining some aspects of religious belief, although avoiding practice except in those liminal moments of life. See Grace Davie, *Religion in Britain Since 1945: Believing Without Belonging* (Malden, MA: Blackwell, 1994).

35. Smith and Denton, *Soul Searching*, 78; Smith and Snell, *Souls in Transition*, 137.

36. Smith and Snell, *Souls in Transition*, 47–48: "Talking about karma does not mean these emerging adults have any real interest in or knowledge about Hinduism, Sikhism, or Buddhism or believe in reincarnation. Nor was it merely a hip shorthand for describing societal social control or divine judgment. Many did not even seem aware of those possible connections. Rather, karma appears to have become a shared, pop culture way of explaining the fair operations of good and bad in the world—among emerging adults, at least. Karma functions as a reminder for emerging adults that they can't get away with bad stuff" (48).

37. Ibid., 51.

38. Ibid., 154.

39. Ibid., 286–87.

40. Christian Smith, "Is Moralistic Therapeutic Deism the New Religion of American Youth?: Implications for the Challenge of Religious Socialization and Reproduction," in *Passing on the Faith: Transforming Traditions for the Next Generation of Jews, Christians, and Muslims*, ed. James Heft (New York: Fordham University Press, 2006), 55–74.

41. Smith and Denton, *Soul Searching*, 162–63.

42. Smith and Snell, *Souls in Transition*, 154–56.

43. Smith and Denton, *Soul Searching*, 169.

44. Christian Smith, "Introduction," 35–36; N. J. Demerath III, "Cultural Victory and Organizational Defeat in the Paradoxical Decline of Liberal Protestantism," *Journal for the Scientific Study of Religion* 34 (1995): 458–69.

45. Smith and Snell, *Souls in Transition*, 288.

46. Ibid., 289.

47. Ibid., 292.

48. Ibid., 146.

49. Ibid., 54.

50. Luigi Giussani, *The Religious Sense*, trans. John Zucchi (Montreal: McGill-Queen's University Press, 1997), 126.

51. Smith and Snell write, "Different religions claim to be unique and do in fact emphasize distinctive ideas and rituals. But ultimately, most emerging adults say, all religions actually share the same core principles, at least those that are important. . . . At heart, in this way all religions are essentially the same, the majority of emerging adults claim, because all religions share the same basic beliefs and values. Therefore, anybody who follows any particular religion is ultimately just like any other religious person following any other religion. People can choose different faiths for themselves, but underneath the different faiths are about the same things. They only differ in their outward appearances and emphases" (*Souls in Transition*, 145).

52. Ibid., 158.

53. Ibid., 52–53.

54. For a theological account of the Ascension, see Douglas Farrow, *Ascension and Ecclesia: On the Significance of the Doctrine of the Ascension for Ecclesiology and Christian Cosmology* (Grand Rapids, MI: Wm. B. Eerdmans, 1999).

55. Smith and Denton, *Soul Searching*, 154.

56. Smith and Snell, *Souls in Transition*, 66–69.

Chapter 3—pages 51–75

1. Portions of the section on Josef Jungmann first appeared as "The Kerygmatic Function of Liturgical Prayer: Liturgical Reform, Meaning, and Identity Formation in the Work of Josef Jungmann," *Studia Liturgica* 41 (2011): 68–77.

2. Josef Jungmann, *The Good News Yesterday and Today,* trans and ed. William A. Huesman (New York: Sadlier, 1962).

3. Ibid., 17.

4. Ibid., 33.

5. Josef Jungmann, *Handing on the Faith: A Manual of Catechetics*, trans. A. N. Fuerst (London: Burns & Oates, 1959), 137–38.

6. Jungmann, *The Good News Yesterday and Today*, 6.

7. Jungmann, *Handing on the Faith*, 397.

8. Jungmann, *The Good News Yesterday and Today*, 26.

9. Josef Jungmann, "The Pastoral Idea in the History of the Liturgy," in *The Assisi Papers: Proceedings of the First International Congress of Pastoral Liturgy* (Collegeville, MN: Liturgical Press, 1957), 23.

10. Josef Jungmann, *The Place of Christ in Liturgical Prayer*, 2nd rev. ed., trans. Geoffrey Chapman (Collegeville, MN: Liturgical Press, 1989).

11. Ibid., 170–71.

12. Ibid., 137.

13. Ibid.

14. Ibid., 139.

15. Jungmann, *The Good News Yesterday and Today*, 115.

16. Josef Jungmann, "The Liturgy, a School of Faith," in *Pastoral Liturgy* (New York: Herder and Herder, 1962), 341.

17. Jungmann, *The Place of Christ in Liturgical Prayer*, 223.

18. Josef Jungmann, "The Defeat of Teutonic Arianism and the Revolution of Religious Culture in the Early Middle Ages," in *Pastoral Liturgy*, 41–42.

19. Jungmann, *The Place of Christ in Liturgical Prayer*, 263.

20. Jungmann, "The Defeat of Teutonic Arianism," 60.

21. Ibid., 2–9.

22. Jungmann, *The Good News Yesterday and Today*, 6–7.

23. Kathleen Hughes, "Jungmann's Influence on Vatican II: Meticulous Scholarship at the Service of a Living Liturgy," in *Source and Summit: Commemorating Josef A. Jungmann, S.J.*, ed. Joanne M. Pierce and Michael Downey (Collegeville, MN: Liturgical Press, 1999), 22.

24. Jungmann, "The Pastoral Idea in the History of the Liturgy," 29.

25. For a summary of these critiques, see John F. Baldovin, *Reforming the Liturgy: A Response to the Critics* (Collegeville, MN: Liturgical Press, 2008), 36–64.

26. Jungmann, *Handing on the Faith*, 98–99.

27. Ibid., 98.

28. Johannes Hofinger, *The Good News and Its Proclamation: Post-Vatican II Edition of the Art of Teaching Christian Doctrine* (Notre Dame, IN: University of Notre Dame Press, 1968), 54.

29. Jungmann, *The Good News Yesterday and Today*, 83.

30. Ibid., 84–85.

31. Ibid., 88–92.

32. Ibid., 103.

33. See Keith Pecklers, *The Unread Vision: The Liturgical Movement in the United States of America 1926–1955* (Collegeville, MN: Liturgical Press, 1998), 8–16.

34. Jungmann, "The Liturgy, A School of Faith," 344.

35. Ibid.

36. Jungmann, *The Good News Yesterday and Today*, 158.

37. Robert Taft, "The Liturgical Year: Studies, Prospects, Reflections," in *Between Memory and Hope: Readings on the Liturgical Year*, ed. Maxwell Johnson (Collegeville: Liturgical Press, 2000), 14.

38. United States Council of Catholic Bishops, *Preaching the Mystery of Faith: The Sunday Homily* (USCCB: Washington DC, 2012), no. 2.

39. Joseph Ratzinger, *Dogma and Preaching: Applying Christian Doctrine to Daily Life*, trans. Matthew J. Miller and Matthew J. O'Connell (San Francisco: Ignatius Press, 2011), 54.

40. For the limitations to historical-critical exegesis and scriptural interpretation, see Matthew Levering, *Participatory Biblical Exegesis: A Theology of Biblical Interpretation* (Notre Dame, IN: University of Notre Dame Press, 2008), 36–62.

41. For an example of such an approach, see Francesca Aran Murphy, *The Comedy of Divine Revelation: Paradise Lost and Regained in Biblical Narrative* (Edinburgh: T. &T. Clark, 2000).

42. Northrop Frye, *The Great Code: The Bible and Literature* (New York: Harcourt Brace, 1982), xiii.

43. Jean-Louis Chrétien, *The Art of Speech*, trans. Andrew Brown (New York: Routledge, 2004), 2–3.

44. Joseph Ratzinger, *Introduction to Christianity*, 2nd ed., trans. Matthew Miller (San Francisco: Ignatius Press, 2004), 128.

45. Joseph Ratzinger, *The God of Jesus Christ: Meditations on the Triune God*, trans. Brian McNeil (San Francisco: Ignatius Press, 2008), 24.

46. Dom Columba Marmion, *Christ in His Mysteries*, trans. Mother M. St. Thomas (St. Louis: Herder, 1939), 29.

47. Augustine, Sermon 191.1 [my translation]. For the full sermon in English, see Augustine, *Sermons,* trans. Edmund Hill, The Works of Saint Augustine III/6 (Hyde Park, NY: New City Press, 1993).

48. Mary Catherine Hilkert, *Naming Grace: Preaching and the Sacramental Imagination* (New York: Continuum, 2002), 49–51.

49. Hans Urs von Balthasar, *Mysterium Paschale: The Mystery of Easter*, trans. Aidan Nichols (San Francisco: Ignatius Press, 2005), 168.

50. Evelyn Underhill, *The School of Charity: Meditations on the Christian Creed* (New York: Longmans, Green, and Co., 1934), 6–7.

51. Portions of this section appeared as "Evangelizing Culture: Cultivating the New Evangelization," *Church Life: A Journal for the New Evangelization* 2, no.1 (2013): 1–4.

52. Melito of Sardis, *On Pascha*, trans. Alistair Stewart-Sykes (Crestwood, NY: St. Vladimir's Seminary Press, 2001).

53. Augustine, Sermon 9, in *Essential Sermons,* ed. Daniel Doyle, trans. Edmund Hill, The Works of Saint Augustine (Hyde Park, NY: New City Press, 2007), 25–43.

54. An introduction to Newman's preaching may be found in *John Henry Newman: Selected Sermons,* ed. Ian Ker (New York: Paulist Press, 1994); also, *Fifteen Sermons Preached Before the University of Oxford* (Notre Dame, IN: University of Notre Dame Press, 1997).

55. Graham Ward, *Cultural Transformation and Religious Practice* (New York: Cambridge University Press, 2005), 5.

56. Paul R. Kolbet, *Augustine and the Cure of Souls: Revising a Classical Ideal,* Christianity and Judaism in Antiquity 17 (Notre Dame, IN: University of Notre Dame Press, 2010), 8–9.

57. Ibid., 40.

58. Graham Ward, "Cultural Hermeneutics and Christian Apologetics," in *Imaginative Apologetics: Theology, Philosophy, and the Catholic Tradition,* ed. Andrew Davison (Grand Rapids: Baker Academic, 2011), 125.

Chapter 4—pages 76–107

1. Edward Hahnenberg, *Awakening Vocation: A Theology of Christian Call* (Collegeville, MN: Liturgical Press, 2010), xiv.

2. Ibid., 226.

3. Mark McIntosh, *Discernment and Truth: The Spirituality and Theology of Knowledge* (New York: Crossroad, 2004), 8.

4. Ibid., 10.

5. Ibid.

6. Ibid., 11–12.

7. Ibid., 12.

8. Augustine, *The Confessions,* trans. Maria Boulding, The Works of Saint Augustine I/1 (Hyde Park, NY: New City Press, 1997), 9.1.1.

9. McIntosh, *Discernment and Truth,* 13.

10. Ibid., 16.

11. Ibid., 17.

12. Ibid., 19.

13. Hans Urs von Balthasar, *Life Out of Death: Meditations on the Paschal Mystery,* trans. Martina Stöckl (San Francisco: Ignatius Press, 2012), 70–71.

14. McIntosh, *Discernment and Truth,* 21.

15. Marilynne Robinson, *Gilead: A Novel* (New York: Farrar, Straus and Giroux, 2004), 245.

16. Dorothy C. Bass and Craig Dykstra, "A Theological Understanding of Christian Practices," in *Practicing Theology: Beliefs and Practices in Christian Life,* ed. Miroslav Volf and Dorothy C. Bass (Grand Rapids, MI: Wm. B. Eerdmans, 2002), 18.

17. Ibid., 22.

18. Ibid., 24.

19. Ibid., 25.

20. Ibid.

21. Ibid., 26.

22. Ibid., 27.

23. *General Instruction of the Roman Missal* 78, accessed June 12, 2013, http://www.usccb.org/prayer-and-worship/the-mass/general-instruction-of-the-roman-missal.

24. Augustine, *Expositions of the Psalms*, vol. 4, ed. John E. Rotelle, trans. Maria Boulding, The Works of Saint Augustine III/18 (Hyde Park, NY: New City Press, 2002), 90(2).13.

25. Thomas Aquinas, *Summa Theologiae* II-II, q. 81, a. 5, ad. 3. English translation from the Fathers of the English Dominican Province.

26. Bryan D. Spinks, *The Sanctus in the Eucharistic Prayer* (New York: Cambridge University Press, 1991), 206. For a summary of theories regarding the historical evolution of the *Sanctus*, see Paul F. Bradshaw and Maxwell E. Johnson, *The Eucharistic Liturgies: Their Evolution and Interpretation* (Collegeville, MN: Liturgical Press, 2012), 111–21.

27. Mitchell, *Meeting Mystery*, 253–54.

28. John D. Laurance, *The Sacrament of the Eucharist*, Lex Orandi Series (Collegeville, MN: Liturgical Press, 2012), 162.

29. For a theological account of the history of the epiclesis, see Yves Congar, *I Believe in the Holy Spirit*, vol. 3, trans. David Smith (New York: Crossroads, 1997), 228–74.

30. Congar, *I Believe in the Holy Spirit*, 3: 271.

31. Chauvet, *Symbol and Sacrament*, 526.

32. Rowan Williams, *Resurrection: Interpreting the Easter Gospel*, 2nd ed. (Cleveland: The Pilgrim Press, 2002), 38.

33. Bradshaw and Johnson, *The Eucharistic Liturgies*, 128.

34. *Catechism of the Catholic Church*, 2nd ed. (Vatican City: Libreria Editrice Vaticana, 2000), no. 1353.

35. Alexander Schmemann, *The Eucharist: Sacrament of the Kingdom*, trans. Paul Kachur (Crestwood, NY: St. Vladimir's Seminary Press, 1987), 200–1.

36. Ratzinger, *God Is With Us*, 86.

37. Ibid., 86–87.

38. Nathan Mitchell, *Cult and Controversy: The Worship of the Eucharist Outside of Mass* (Collegeville, MN: Liturgical Press, 1982), 426.

39. Laurance, *The Sacrament of the Eucharist*, 167.

40. Evelyn Underhill, *The Mystery of Sacrifice: A Meditation on the Liturgy* (New York: Longmans, Green, and Co, 1938), 22–23.

41. David W. Fagerberg, *On Liturgical Asceticism* (Washington, DC: The Catholic University Press, 2013).

42. Corbon, *The Wellspring of Worship*, 154.

43. Underhill, *The Mystery of Sacrifice*, 33–34.

44. David Power, *Sacrament: The Language of God's Giving* (New York: Crossroad, 1999), 168–69.

45. Jacques Maritain and Raïssa Maritain, *Liturgy and Contemplation*, trans. Joseph W. Evans (New York: P. J. Kenedy & Sons, 1960), 31.

46. Augustine, *The City of God*, 22.30 [my translation].

47. Flannery O'Connor, "Revelation," in *The Complete Short Stories* (New York: Farrar, Straus and Giroux, 1971), 508.

Chapter 5—pages 108–33

1. Joseph Ratzinger, *The Spirit of the Liturgy*, trans. John Saward (San Francisco: Ignatius Press, 2000), 32–33.

2. Ibid., 33.

3. Joseph Ratzinger, *'In the Beginning . . .': A Catholic Understanding of the Story of Creation and the Fall*, trans. Boniface Ramsey (Grand Rapids, MI: Eerdmans, 1995), 48.

4. Ibid., 70–71.

5. Ibid., 76.

6. Gregory Dix, *The Image and Likeness of God* (London: Dacre Press, 1953), 43–62.

7. Bruce T. Morrill, *Divine Worship and Human Healing: Liturgical Theology at the Margins of Life and Death* (Collegeville, MN: Liturgical Press, 2009), 166.

8. David Bentley Hart, *The Beauty of the Infinite: The Aesthetics of Christian Truth* (Grand Rapids, MI: Eerdmans, 2003), 351.

9. George Herbert, "Love (3)," in *George Herbert: The Complete English Poems*, ed. John Tobin (New York: Penguin, 1991), 178.

10. Robin M. Jensen, *Baptismal Imagery in Early Christianity: Ritual, Visual, and Theological Dimensions* (Grand Rapids, MI: Baker Academic, 2012).

11. Ann W. Astell, *Eating Beauty: The Eucharist and the Spiritual Arts of the Middle Ages* (Ithaca, NY: Cornell University Press, 2006); Miri Rubin, *Corpus Christi: The Eucharist in Late Medieval Culture* (New York: Cambridge University Press, 1991).

12. Roberto S. Goizueta, *Caminemos Con Jesús: Toward a Hispanic/Latino Theology of Accompaniment* (Maryknoll, NY: Orbis Books, 1995), 103–11.

13. Horton Davies, *Worship and Theology in England From Watts and Wesley to Martineau, 1690–1900*, vol. 3 (Grand Rapids, MI: Eerdmans, 1996), 278–79.

14. Brenna Moore, *Sacred Dread: Raïssa Maritain, the Allure of Suffering, and the French Catholic Revival (1905–1944)* (Notre Dame, IN: University of Notre Dame Press, 2013), 123–48.

15. John Tavener, *The Music of Silence: A Composer's Testament*, ed. Brian Keeble (New York: Faber and Faber, 1999), 176–82.

16. Cecilia González-Andrieu, *Bridge to Wonder: Art as a Gospel of Beauty* (Waco, TX: Baylor University Press, 2012), 56–57.

17. Hans Urs von Balthasar, *The Glory of the Lord: A Theological Aesthetics, Volume 1: Seeing the Form*, trans. Erasmo Leiva-Merikakis (San Francisco: Ignatius Press, 1982), 124.

18. Hart, *The Beauty of the Infinite*, 28.

19. See John Donne, "Christ the Light," in *John Donne: Selections from Divine Poems, Sermons, Devotions, and Prayers*, ed. John Booty (New York: Paulist Press, 1990), 119–36.

20. Duncan Stroik, "Can We Afford Not to Build Beautiful Churches?," in *The Church Building as a Sacred Place: Beauty, Transcendence, and the Eternal* (Chicago: Hillenbrand, 2012), 111.

21. Denis R. McNamara, *Catholic Church Architecture and the Spirit of the Liturgy* (Chicago: Hillenbrand Books, 2009), 143.

22. Ibid., 69.

23. Power, *Sacrament*, 72–73.

24. Ratzinger, *The Spirit of the Liturgy*, 150.

25. Anthony Ruff, *Sacred Music and Liturgical Reform: Treasures and Transformations* (Chicago: Hillenbrand Books, 2007), 563–602.

26. Hart, *The Beauty of the Infinite*, 298.

27. Samuel J. Stone, "The Church's One Foundation," in *The Hymnal of the Protestant Episcopal Church in the United States of America 1940* (New York: The Church Pension Fund, 1961), 396.

28. William A. Dyrness, *Poetic Theology: God and the Poetics of Everyday Life* (Grand Rapids, MI: Wm. B. Eerdmans, 2011), 85.

29. Alejandro García-Rivera, *The Community of the Beautiful: A Theological Aesthetics* (Collegeville, MN: Liturgical Press, 1999), 169.

30. Hans Urs von Balthasar, *Seeing the Form*, 253.

31. John Henry Newman, "Worship, a Preparation for Christ's Coming (Advent)," in *Selected Sermons*, 284–85.

32. Christian Smith with Kari Christoffersen, Hilary Davidson, and Patricia Snell Herzog, *Lost in Transition: The Dark Side of Emerging Adulthood* (New York: Oxford University Press, 2011), 238.

Bibliography

Documents

Benedict XVI. *Sacramentum Caritatis*. Boston: Pauline Books, 2007.

————. *Verbum Domini*. Boston: Pauline Books, 2010.

Catechism of the Catholic Church. 2nd ed. Vatican City: Libreria Editrice Vaticana, 2000.

Flannery, Austin, ed. *Vatican Council II: Constitutions, Decrees, Declarations*. Northport, NY: Costello Publishing, 1996.

The General Instruction of the Roman Missal. Revised edition. Washington, DC: USCCB Publishing, 2011.

John Paul II. *Catechesi Tradendae*. Washington, DC: USCCB Publishing, 1979.

————. *Redemptoris Missio*. Boston: Pauline Books, 1990.

————. *Redemptor Hominis*. New York: Pauline Books, 2009.

Paul VI. *Evangelium Nuntiandi*. In *The Catechetical Documents: A Parish Resource*, edited by Martin Connell, 149–200. Chicago: Liturgical Training Publications, 1996.

The Rites of the Catholic Church. Vol. 1. Collegeville, MN: Liturgical Press, 1990.

United States Council of Catholic Bishops (USCCB). *General Directory for Catechesi*. Washington, DC: USCCB Publishing, 1997.

————. *National Directory for Catechesis*. Washington, DC: USCCB Publishing, 2005.

————. *Preaching the Mystery of Faith*. Washington, DC: USCCB Publishing, 2013.

Additional Works

Aquinas, Thomas. *The Summa Theologica of St. Thomas Aquinas*. Translated by the Fathers of the Dominican Province. Notre Dame, IN: Christian Classics, 1948.

Astell, Ann W. *Eating Beauty: The Eucharist and the Spiritual Arts of the Middle Ages*. Ithaca, NY: Cornell University Press, 2006.

Augustine. *The Confessions*. Translated by Maria Boulding. The Works of Saint Augustine I/1. Hyde Park, NY: New City Press, 1997.

————. *The City of God Against the Pagans*. Translated by R. W. Dyson. New York: Cambridge University Press, 1998.

————. *Expositions of the Psalms*. Vol. 4. Translated by Maria Boulding. The Works of Saint Augustine III/18. Hyde Park, NY: New City Press, 2002.

Baldovin, John F. *Reforming the Liturgy: A Response to the Critics*. Collegeville, MN: Liturgical Press, 2008.

Balthasar, Hans Urs von. *The Glory of the Lord: A Theological Aesthetics*. Vol. 1, *Seeing the Form*. Translated by Erasmo Leiva-Merikakis. San Francisco: Ignatius Press, 1982.

————. *Love Alone Is Credible*. Translated by D. C. Schindler. San Francisco: Ignatius Press, 2004.

————. *Mysterium Paschale: The Mystery of Easter*. Translated by Aidan Nichols. San Francisco: Ignatius Press, 2005.

————. *Life Out of Death: Meditations on the Paschal Mystery*. Translated by Martina Stöckl. San Francisco: Ignatius Press, 2012.

Bass, Dorothy, and Craig Dykstra. "A Theological Understanding of Christian Practices." In *Practicing Theology: Beliefs and Practice in Christian Life*, edited by Miroslav Volf and Dorothy C. Bass, 13–32. Grand Rapids, MI: Wm. B. Eerdmans, 2002.

Bellah, Robert, et al. *Habits of the Heart: Individualism and Commitment in American Life*. 3rd ed. Berkeley, CA: University of California Press, 2008.

Bouyer, Louis. *The Liturgy Revived: A Doctrinal Commentary of the Conciliar Constitution on the Liturgy*. Notre Dame, IN: University of Notre Dame Press, 1964.

————. *The Church of God: Body of Christ and Temple of the Spirit*. Translated by Charles Underhill Quinn. San Francisco: Ignatius Press, 2011.

Bradshaw, Paul F., and Maxwell E. Johnson. *The Eucharistic Liturgies: Their Evolution and Interpretation*. Collegeville, MN: Liturgical Press, 2012.

Burgaleta, Claudio M. "Benedict XVI and the New Evangelization." *Church Life: A Journal for the New Evangelization* 2 (2013): 55–60.

Casanova, José. *Public Religions in the Modern World*. Chicago: The University of Chicago Press, 1994.

Casel, Odo. *The Mystery of Christian Worship*. Edited by Burkhard Neunheuser. New York: Crossroad, 1962.

Chrétien, Jean-Louis. *The Art of Speech*. Translated by Andrew Brown. New York: Routledge, 2004.

Congar, Yves. *I Believe in the Holy Spirit*. Vol. 3. Translated by David Smith. New York: Crossroad, 1997.

————. *The Meaning of Tradition*. Translated by A. N. Woodrow. San Francisco: Ignatius Press, 2004.

————. "The *Ecclesia* or Christian Community as a Whole Celebrates the Liturgy." In *At the Heart of Christian Worship: Liturgical Essays by Yves Congar*, translated and edited by Paul Philibert, 15–68. Collegeville, MN: Liturgical Press, 2010.

Corbon, Jean. *The Wellspring of Worship*. Translated by Matthew J. O'Connell. San Francisco: Ignatius Press, 2005.

Davie, Grace. *Religion in Britain Since 1945: Believing Without Belonging*. Malden, MA: Blackwell, 1994.

———. *Europe—The Exceptional Case: Parameters of Faith in the Modern World*. London: Darton, Longman & Todd, 2002.

Davies, Horton. *Worship and Theology in England From Watts and Wesley to Martineau, 1690–1900*. Vol. 3. Grand Rapids, MI: Wm. B. Eerdmans, 1996.

de Lubac, Henri. *Catholicism: Christ and the Common Destiny of Man*. Translated by Lancelot C. Sheppard and Elizabeth Englund. San Francisco: Ignatius Press, 1988.

Demerath III, N. J. "Cultural Victory and Organizational Defeat in the Paradoxical Decline of Liberal Protestantism." *Journal for the Scientific Study of Religion* 34, no. 4 (1995): 458–69.

Dix, Gregory. *The Image and Likeness of God*. London: Dacre Press, 1953.

Donne, John. *John Donne: Selections from Divine Poems, Sermons, Devotions, and Prayers*. Edited by John Booty. New York: Paulist Press, 1990.

Dyrness, William A. *Poetic Theology: God and the Poetics of Everyday Life*. Grand Rapids, MI: Wm. B. Eerdmans, 2011.

Fagerberg, David W. *On Liturgical Asceticism*. Washington DC: The Catholic University of America Press, 2013.

Faggioli, Massimo. *True Reform: Liturgy and Ecclesiology in Sacrosanctum Concilium*. Collegeville, MN: Liturgical Press, 2012.

Farrow, Douglas. *Ascension and Ecclesia: On the Significance of the Doctrine of the Ascension for Ecclesiology and Christian Cosmology*. Grand Rapids, MI: Wm. B. Eerdmans, 1999.

Frye, Northrop. *The Great Code: The Bible and Literature*. New York: Harcourt Brace, 1982.

Fuller, Robert C. *Spiritual But Not Religious: Understanding Unchurched America*. New York: Oxford University Press, 2001.

García-Rivera, Alejandro. *The Community of the Beautiful: A Theological Aesthetics*. Collegeville, MN: Liturgical Press, 1999.

Giuissani, Luigi. *The Religious Sense*. Translated by John Zucchi. Montreal: McGill–Queen's University Press, 1997.

Goizueta, Roberto S. *Caminemos Con Jesús: Toward a Hispanic/Latino Theology of Accompaniment*. Maryknoll, NY: Orbis Books, 1995.

González-Andrieu, Cecilia. *Bride to Wonder: Art as a Gospel of Beauty*. Waco, TX: Baylor University Press, 2012.

Habermas, Jürgen, and Joseph Ratzinger. *The Dialectics of Secularization: On Reason and Religion*. San Francisco: Ignatius Press, 2006.

Hahnenberg, Edward. *Awakening Vocation: A Theology of Christian Call*. Collegeville, MN: Liturgical Press, 2010.

Hart, David Bentley. *The Beauty of the Infinite: The Aesthetics of Christian Truth*. Grand Rapids, MI: Wm. B. Eerdmans, 2003.

Herbert, George. *The Complete English Poems*. Edited by John Tobin. New York: Penguin Books, 1991.

Hilkert, Mary Catherine. *Naming Grace: Preaching and the Sacramental Imagination*. New York: Continuum, 2002.

Hofinger, Johannes. *The Good News and Its Proclamation: Post-Vatican II Edition of the Art of Teaching Christian Doctrine*. Notre Dame, IN: University of Notre Dame Press, 1968.

Hughes, Kathleen. "Jungmann's Influence on Vatican II: Meticulous Scholarship at the Service of a Living Liturgy." In *Source and Summit: Commemorating Josef A. Jungmann, S.J.*, edited by Joanne M. Pierce and Michael Downey. Collegeville, MN: Liturgical Press, 1999.

Jackson, Pamela. *An Abundance of Graces: Reflections on* Sacrosanctum Concilium. Chicago: Hillenbrand Books, 2004.

Jensen, Robin M. *Baptismal Imagery in Early Christianity: Ritual, Visual, and Theological Dimensions*. Grand Rapids, MI: Baker Academic, 2012.

Jungmann, Josef. "The Pastoral Idea in the History of the Liturgy." In *The Assisi Papers: Proceedings of the First International Congress of Pastoral Liturgy*, 223–36. Collegeville, MN: Liturgical Press, 1956.

———. *Handing on the Faith: A Manual of Catechetics*. Translated by A. N. Fuerst. London: Burns & Oates, 1959.

———. "The Defeat of Teutonic Arianism and the Revolution of Religious Culture in the Early Middle Ages." In *Pastoral Liturgy*, 1–101. New York: Herder and Herder, 1962.

———. *The Good News Yesterday and Today*. Translated by William A. Huesman. New York: Sadlier, 1962.

———. "The Liturgy, a School of Faith." In *Pastoral Liturgy*, 334–44. New York: Herder and Herder, 1962.

———. "Constitution on the Sacred Liturgy." Translated by Lalit Adolphus. In *Commentary on the Documents of Vatican II,* edited by Herbert Vorgrimler, 1:1–87. New York: Herder and Herder, 1967.

———. *The Place of Christ in Liturgical Prayer*. 2nd rev. ed. Translated by Geoffrey Chapman. Collegeville, MN: Liturgical Press, 1989.

Kolbet, Paul. *Augustine and the Cure of Souls: Revising a Classical Ideal*. Notre Dame, IN: University of Notre Dame Press, 2010.

Laurance, John D. *The Sacrament of the Eucharist*. Lex Orandi Series. Collegeville, MN: Liturgical Press, 2012.

Levering, Matthew. *Participatory Biblical Exegesis: A Theology of Biblical Interpretation*. Notre Dame, IN: University of Notre Dame Press, 2008.

Maritain, Jacques, and Raïssa Maritain. *Liturgy and Contemplation*. Translated by Joseph W. Evans. New York: P. J. Kenedy & Sons, 1960.

Marmion, Dom Columba. *Christ in His Mysteries*. Translated by Mother M. St. Thomas. St. Louis: Herder, 1939.

Martin, David. *On Secularization: Toward a Revised General Theory.* Burlington, VT: Ashgate, 2005.

McIntosh, Mark. *Discernment and Truth: The Spirituality and Theology of Knowledge.* New York: Crossroad, 2004.

McNamara, Denis R. *Catholic Church Architecture and the Spirit of the Liturgy.* Chicago: Hillenbrand Books, 2009.

Melito of Sardis. *On Pascha.* Translated by Alistair Steward-Sykes. Crestwood, NY: St. Vladimir's Seminary Press, 2001.

Mitchell, Nathan. *Cult and Controversy: The Worship of the Eucharist Outside of Mass.* New York: Pueblo Publishing, 1982.

———. *Meeting Mystery: Liturgy, Worship, Sacraments.* Maryknoll, NY: Orbis Books, 2006.

Moore, Brenna. *Sacred Dread: Raïssa Maritain, the Allure of Suffering, and the French Catholic Revival (1905–1944).* Notre Dame, IN: University of Notre Dame Press, 2013.

Morrill, Bruce. *Divine Worship and Human Healing: Liturgical Theology at the Margins of Life and Death.* Collegeville, MN: Liturgical Press, 2009.

———. *Encountering Christ in the Eucharist: The Paschal Mystery in People, Word, and Sacrament.* New York: Paulist Press, 2012.

Mouroux, Jean. *The Christian Experience: An Introduction to Theology.* Translated by George Lamb. New York: Sheed and Ward, 1954.

Murphy, Francesca Aran. *The Comedy of Divine Revelation: Paradise Lost and Regained in Biblical Narrative.* Edinburgh: T. & T. Clark, 2000.

Newman, John Henry. *John Henry Newman: Selected Sermons.* Edited by Ian Ker. New York: Paulist Press, 1994.

———. *Fifteen Sermons Preached Before the University of Oxford.* Notre Dame: University of Notre Dame Press, 1997.

O'Brien, David J., and Thomas A. Shannon, eds. *Catholic Social Thought: A Documentary Heritage.* Maryknoll, NY: Orbis Books, 2010.

O'Connor, Flannery. *The Complete Stories.* New York: Farrar, Straus and Giroux, 1971.

O'Malley, Timothy. "The Kerygmatic Function of Liturgical Prayer: Liturgical Reform, Meaning, and Identity Formation in the Work of Josef Jungmann." *Studia Liturgica* 41 (2011): 68–77.

———. "Evangelizing Culture: Cultivating the New Evangelization," *Church Life: A Journal for the New Evangelization* 2, no.1 (2013): 1–4.

Pecklers, Keith. *The Unread Vision: The Liturgical Movement in the United States of America 1926–1955.* Collegeville, MN: Liturgical Press, 1998.

Power, David N. *Sacrament: The Language of God's Giving.* New York: Crossroad, 1999.

Ratzinger, Joseph. *'In the Beginning . . .': A Catholic Understanding of the Story of Creation and the Fall.* Translated by Boniface Ramsey. Grand Rapids, MI: Wm. B. Eerdmans, 1990.

————. *The Spirit of the Liturgy*. Translated by John Saward. San Francisco: Ignatius Press, 2000.

————. *God Is Near Us: The Eucharist, the Heart of Life*. Edited by Stephan Otto Horn and Vinzenze Pfnür. Translated by Henry Taylor. San Francisco: Ignatius Press, 2003.

————. *Introduction to Christianity*. 2nd ed. Translated by Matthew Miller. San Francisco: Ignatius Press, 2004.

————. *Pilgrim Fellowship of Faith: The Church as Communion*. Edited by Stephan Otto Horn and Vinzenze Pfnür. Translated by Henry Taylor. San Francisco: Ignatius Press, 2005.

————. *The God of Jesus Christ: Meditations on the Triune God*. Translated by Brian McNeil. San Francisco: Ignatius Press, 2008.

————. *Dogma and Preaching: Applying Christian Doctrine to Daily Life*. Translated by Michael J. Miller and Matthew J. O'Connell. San Francisco: Ignatius Press, 2011.

Robinson, Marilynne. *Gilead: A Novel*. New York: Farrar, Straus and Giroux, 2004.

Rubin, Miri. *Corpus Christi: The Eucharist in Late Medieval Culture*. New York: Cambridge University Press, 1991.

Ruff, Anthony. *Sacred Music and Liturgical Reform: Treasures and Transformations*. Chicago: Hillenbrand Books, 2007.

Schmemann, Alexander. *The Eucharist: Sacrament of the Kingdom*. Translated by Paul Kachur. Crestwood, NY: St. Vladimir's Seminary Press, 1987.

Searle, Mark. "Infant Baptism Reconsidered." In *Living Water, Sealing Spirit: Readings on Christian Initiation*, edited by Maxwell Johnson, 365–409. Collegeville, MN: Liturgical Press, 1995.

Smith, Christian. "Introduction." In *The Secular Revolution: Power, Interests, and Conflict in the Secularization of American Public Life*, edited by Christian Smith, 1–96. Berkeley, CA: University of California Press, 2003.

————, with Melissa Lundquist. *Soul Searching: The Religious and Spiritual Lives of American Teenagers*. New York: Oxford University Press, 2005.

————. "Is Moralistic Therapeutic Deism the New Religion of American Youth? Implications for the Challenge of Religious Socialization and Reproduction." In *Passing on the Faith: Transforming Traditions for the Next Generation of Jews, Christians, and Muslims*, edited by James Heft, 55–74. New York: Fordham University Press, 2006.

————, with Patricia Snell. *Souls in Transition: The Religious and Spiritual Lives of Emerging Adults*. New York: Oxford University Press, 2009.

————. *What Is a Person?: Rethinking Humanity, Social Life, and the Moral Good from the Person Up*. Chicago: University of Chicago Press, 2010.

————, with Kari Christoffersen, Hilary Davidson, and Patricia Snell Herzog. *Lost in Transition: The Dark Side of Emerging Adulthood*. New York: Oxford University Press, 2011.

Spinks, Bryan D. *The Sanctus in the Eucharistic Prayer*. New York: Cambridge University Press, 1991.

Stone, Samuel J. "The Church's One Foundation." In *The Hymnal of the Protestant Episcopal Church in the United States of America 1940.* New York: The Church Pension Fund, 1961.

Stroik, Duncan G. *The Church Building as a Sacred Place: Beauty, Transcendence, and the Eternity.* Chicago: Hillenbrand Books, 2009.

Taft, Robert. "The Liturgical Year: Studies, Prospects, Reflections." In *Between Memory and Hope: Readings on the Liturgical Year*, edited by Maxwell E. Johnson, 3–24. Collegeville, MN: Liturgical Press, 2000.

Tavener, John. *The Music of Silence: A Composer's Testament.* Edited by Brian Keeble. New York: Faber and Faber, 1999.

Taylor, Charles. *A Secular Age.* Cambridge, MA: Belknap Press, 2009.

———. *Dilemmas and Connections: Selected Essays.* Cambridge, MA: Belknap Press, 2011.

Tillard, J.-M.-R. *Flesh of the Church, Flesh of Christ: At the Source of the Ecclesiology of Communion.* Collegeville, MN: Liturgical Press, 2001.

Underhill, Evelyn. *The School of Charity: Meditations on the Christian Creed.* New York: Longmans, Green, and Co., 1934.

———. *The Mystery of Sacrifice: A Meditation on the Liturgy.* New York: Longmans, Green, and Co., 1938.

Vagaggini, Cyprian. *Theological Dimensions of the Liturgy: A General Treatise on the Theology of the Liturgy.* 4th ed. Translated by Leonard J. Doyle and W. A. Jurgens. Collegeville, MN: Liturgical Press, 1976.

Wainwright, Geoffrey. *Doxology: The Praise of God in Worship, Doctrine, and Life.* New York: Oxford University Press, 1980.

Ward, Graham. *Cultural Transformation and Religious Practice.* New York: Cambridge University Press, 2005.

———. "Cultural Hermeneutics and Christian Apologetics." In *Imaginative Apologetics: Theology, Philosophy, and the Catholic Tradition*, edited by Andrew Davison, 115–25. Grand Rapids, MI: Baker Academic, 2011.

Williams, Rowan. *Resurrection: Interpreting the Easter Gospel.* 2nd ed. Cleveland: The Pilgrim Press, 2002.